PENGUIN BOOKS

THE SEWING ROOM

Barbara Cawthorne Crafton is an Episcopal priest whose work has ranged from Trinity Church on Wall Street to the New York City waterfront. She currently serves on the staff of Seamen's Church Institute, an organization serving merchant seafarers. Her essays have appeared in such places as *New Woman*, *Family Circle*, and the "Hers" column of *The New York Times Magazine*.

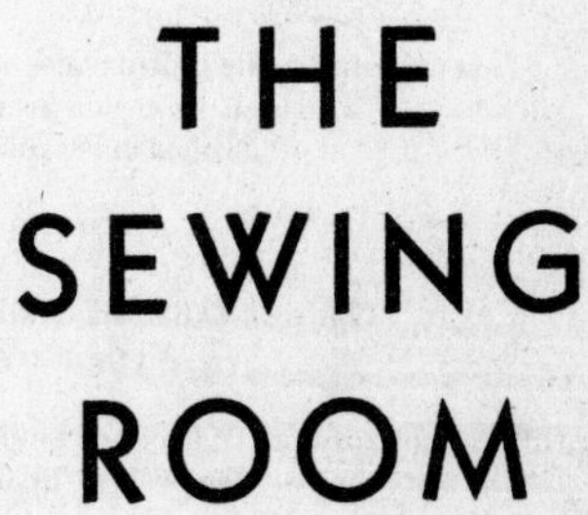

THE SEWING ROOM

BARBARA CAWTHORNE CRAFTON

PENGUIN BOOKS

CANA LIBRARY
BERKLEY, MICHIGAN

814.54
Cra
2021 6/28/94 Gift

PENGUIN BOOKS
Published by the Penguin Group
Penguin Books USA Inc., 375 Hudson Street, New York, New York 10014, U.S.A.
Penguin Books Ltd, 27 Wrights Lane, London W8 5TZ, England
Penguin Books Australia Ltd, Ringwood, Victoria, Australia
Penguin Books Canada Ltd, 10 Alcorn Avenue, Toronto, Ontario, Canada M4V 3B2
Penguin Books (N.Z.) Ltd, 182–190 Wairau Road, Auckland 10, New Zealand

Penguin Books Ltd, Registered Offices: Harmondsworth, Middlesex, England

First published in the United States of America by Viking Penguin,
a division of Penguin Books USA Inc., 1993
Published in Penguin Books 1994

1 3 5 7 9 10 8 6 4 2

Copyright © Barbara Cawthorne Crafton, 1993
All rights reserved

"Showing Off" first appeared as "Of Lace and Little Women" in *Journal of Women's Ministries*; "The Girls" in *New Woman*; and "Up to Whitby" in *Books & Religion*.
"The Sewing Room" was published under the title "Reap What You Sew" in *The New York Times Magazine*. Copyright © 1990 by The New York Times Company. Reprinted by permission. "The Second Time Around" was published as "Happily Ever After" in *Family Circle*. Reprinted with permission. © 1989 The Family Circle Inc.

Grateful acknowledgment is made for permission to reprint the excerpt on page 253 from "Love Me Tender" by Elvis Presley and Vera Matson. Copyright © 1956 by Elvis Presley Music, Inc. Copyright renewed and assigned to Elvis Presley Music (administered by R&H Music). International copyright secured. All rights reserved.

THE LIBRARY OF CONGRESS HAS CATALOGUED THE HARDCOVER AS FOLLOWS:
Crafton, Barbara Cawthorne.
The sewing room: uncommon reflections on life, love, and work/Barbara Cawthorne Crafton.
p. cm.
ISBN 0-670-84113-7 (hc.)
ISBN 0 14 01.5830 8 (pbk.)
1. Life. 2. Crafton, Barbara Cawthorne. I. Title.
BD431.C78 1993
814′.54—dc20 92-12149

Printed in the United States of America
Set in Bodoni Book
Designed by Brian Mulligan

Except in the United States of America, this book is sold subject to the condition that it shall not, by way of trade or otherwise, be lent, re-sold, hired out, or otherwise circulated without the publisher's prior consent in any form of binding or cover other than that in which it is published and without a similar condition including this condition being imposed on the subsequent purchaser.

TO WILL MCCORMACK

ACKNOWLEDGMENTS

A number of people have been kind enough to test-drive one or more of these stories, or to appear in them. I thank all of them: Mary Jones; Carol Towt; Jack Moody; Sara Waterbury; Carlyle Windley; that dreadful Bly woman; Katherine Kurs; Sue Reel; Slone Stambaugh; Kate Williams; Jim Whittemore; Gibbi Cox; Brother Justus; John Tormey; Stuart Green; Caroline Stacey; Cathy Burdick; Mary S. McCormack; Bridget W. B. McCormack; Chris Davenport; Noah; Win Peacock; Jennifer Barrows; Joan Tappan; Greg Barr; David Jette; Barbara Clauson; Lisa Biro; Natalie Harding; Barbara Davison; the homeless people of lower Manhattan, especially the clients of John Heuss House; the seafarers of the world, wherever they may be; Robin and Linda and the Girl Scouts; the men of Saint Paul's Shelter; Pat Burton-Eadie; Monty Roberts; Carol Stevenson; Deener and Dan Matthews; the Compassionate Friends; all the people of Saint Luke's; and the people of Trinity Church. And Carla Glasser. And Mindy Werner from Viking. And my parents, all three of them. And my five favorite people: Rosie, Madeline, Corinna, Anna, and Q. Love never ends.

—BCC

New York City

1992

ACKNOWLEDGMENTS

[illegible]

CONTENTS

INTRODUCTION

PEOPLE ARE WHAT MATTER. If you're setting up a newspaper page, you know that you need to have pictures of people on page one. Not landscapes. Not buildings. Those things don't interest most of us for very long. What we search the photographs for are faces: people talking to each other, people angry at one another, people kissing each other, even people killing each other. And we search the faces: What is he thinking as he smiles at her? What is it like to be that young soldier? Or his mother? Or the president of the United States? What's behind the expressionless face of the accused as she attends her own arraignment?

People are what matter. I sit in a group of homeless people who meet in a church basement to drink coffee and talk about their lives. One man, new to the group, speaks for the first time. He has no home. He has no place to take a shower and his smell supports that claim. He has had no breakfast. He is addicted to alcohol. He has no money. He has no job. And what does he talk about? He talks about his family when he was young, about an older brother who outshone him, about not measuring up. With all these things going wrong in his life today, the thing that comes out of his mouth is about the people he first loved. About caring what they thought. About longing for their attention and approval. After all these years.

I'm the same way. Everything comes back to people: people I love, people I've disappointed, people I worry about, people I mourn. Buildings are interesting because people talked and flirted and lived and died in them. An old ball gown in a museum was worn by someone who studied herself in a mirror and thought about what might happen on a tonight two hundred years ago. Who was she? My old photographs, my children's old dresses, my term papers from college—they are junk. But I cannot get rid of them. They are my life.

This book is a string of people's moments: snapshots of diverse people in many different situations who nonetheless all have said something to me about my own life. And to you about yours, I hope. Like you, I meet them all over. So that you won't be confused as you graze through the book, here are some of the places we will be:

We'll be at home, trying to make sense of what on earth family means these days. And what it meant when we were little. I'm a mom—I've been in the trenches for twenty-five years. If you have, too, you know it's not for sissies. Neither is being a wife. I understand being a husband is challenging as well.

We'll be at work. I don't know what you do for a living, but whatever it is, you spend most of your waking hours doing it. So it's got to matter. I'm an Episcopal priest myself, and have been that odd thing in lots of different places: on the waterfront, in a happy suburban parish, in a large urban church. So we'll be calling on people in hospitals, in homeless shelters, on ships. Wear old clothes.

Then we'll visit some other places. You can't work all the time.

THE SEWING ROOM

THE SEWING ROOM

I HAVE TAKEN OVER a basement room in which someone who lived here before left a Ping-Pong table. It is now my sewing room. The table is just the right height for me, and I can spread out the fabric on its expanse of dark green when I cut things out. It's cool there in the summer, and quiet. I listen to the radio and work away, and a flat piece of cloth takes on shape as I work, grows breast-shaped curves and hips, gathers itself into a waistband, to which I have added an inch because I am fatter than I wish I were.

This activity uses resources seldom called upon in the rest of my life. Beyond basic decisions about color, style, and fabric, there is little thought involved in sewing. Clothing construction follows the same rules whatever the garment. You sew a seam and finish the edges. Right sides go together unless it says otherwise. You press seams open, and darts toward the center or down. You do not argue with the seams about the degree of their openness, nor do you seek a dart consensus about which way *they* want to be pressed. There are virtually no moral ambiguities in sewing.

The outcome of a sewing project is never uncertain. I know in advance exactly what I will get, and I control all phases of production. When I finish, I can point to what I have made. In fact, I can *wear* what I have made, or put it on my granddaughter and watch *her* parade in it. I can imagine my image of myself, or of her, and then I can make it real.

None of this bears much resemblance to the way I earn my living, which is by having meetings and deciding about things and evaluating things. And compromising about things, acting in situations in which I know in advance I won't get all I want. And talking to people on the phone. And listening patiently as people tell me things I already know.

After a week of this, I am ready for a change. I go down the basement stairs, feeling the earthen coolness coming up to meet me as I descend. And there in the sewing room is my brand-new machine, gleaming white in the dark. Hello. Tough week? Never mind—let's make something, shall we?

I learned to sew on an ancestor of this sleek white beauty. She was black enameled steel. She had beautiful gold filigree decorations, and an iron treadle attached to her balance wheel, which you ran with alternating feet instead of with a motor. She sewed forward and backward, period. She lived in a mahogany cabinet built just for her, and she was anything but portable.

The sewing machine was upstairs in my grandmother's sewing room, one of the attic rooms in the gable-crazed house we lived in when I was a girl. Bits of fabric, rickrack, short pieces of lace, and spools of thread were everywhere. The linoleum was gray with yellow and pink flowers; here and there, a dropped straight pin gleamed against it. Here my grandmother sat and made beautiful things. And she taught me.

Back and forth I would sew, struggling to get the rhythm of the pedals right so the wheel would turn smoothly. Learning to pivot. Learning to sew a curved line. Learning to make a dart. Learning to insert a zipper—two ways. Making mistakes and showing them to her. Ripping them out and redoing the work. And getting it right. My grandmother's eyes, with their crinkles at the sides. Her smile at my intentness, a smile whose dimple was still beguiling even though she was old. And her stories, while we worked, about the Swedish people in Minnesota where we came from, about her brothers and sisters. About my mother when she was little. The attic room must have been hot in those pre-air-conditioned days, but I don't remember it so. I remember it as a place of beauty and peace.

After my grandmother died and we moved, my parents bought me a sewing machine of my very own. She was electric. Though her body was also steel, it was not black with filigree but tan. Where her forerunner had feminine curves, she was streamlined, like the cars of her era. She sewed forward and backward, of course, but she also made zigzags, large ones or small ones, fine enough to finish a buttonhole. She could blind hem, catching up just a thread of a skirt and keeping the visible work on the underside where nobody could see. She was portable if one were young and strong.

In the new house we had no sewing room. I sat in my bedroom and made rebellious clothes. Bell-bottom trousers with plate-size flowers in red, white, and blue. Hip-hugger miniskirts with wide belts. Granny dresses, with high waists and necks, in which I hoped to look like I was from London. No more summer stories about Scandinavian people in the Midwest: now the needle thump-thumped to the Beatles, to the Rolling Stones, to the Supremes, to the Beach Boys. Yeah.

But I didn't just sew for myself. I also sewed for my mother. It skips a generation, my grandmother used to say, and in our family that was true. When she grew too old to sew for my mother, I was old enough to start. My mother never learned. And so the bell-bottoms and granny dresses were interspersed with other things: A bottle-green silk suit with lime-green lapels and a blouse to match. A pink silk nightgown with lace trim, which she left in a hotel once and mourned as long as she lived. A gray shirtdress with silver buttons. A white cape with gold ones. And later my daughters joined the sorority: A christening dress with twenty yards of embroidered ruffles. A green corduroy jumper with mushroom appliqués. A lavender gingham sundress with embroidered butterflies. A velvet Christmas dress with red cherry trim. Corduroy overalls with giant rickrack around the neck and waist, the inner legs closed with snaps for quick diaper changes.

But gradually my production slowed to a trickle, and then it stopped. The pursuit of professional competence and my desire to succeed left many gentle nourishments in the dust. Marriage was one. Sewing was another. The tan, streamlined beauty whose hum had accompanied so many parts of my life lay, unoiled and unused, on the closet floor. I didn't have time. And I didn't want to have time. My feminist politics seemed to put her in a new and unflattering light. She seemed to abet the embroidering of unnecessary tasks that were better bought than performed. I was a thinker, a leader, and a doer. I unconsciously billed myself by the hour for everything I did, computing the "real" cost of everything. I was too busy to cook—we ate out a lot. We moved to a condominium, where someone else would do the maintenance while I did my important work. It no longer seemed a wise use of my time to sew. And so one day I put my friend out with the trash.

How could I have done that to the partner of my youth? I was busy. I was tired. I was full of the demand that I do well in a career that had been, for a long time, a men-only one. I was able, in the energetic and rewarding pursuit of my profession, to avoid my disappointment at my own failures. And so I didn't want to be around my old friend. She knew too much.

But years pass again, and life changes. Love comes again. Marriage. My youngest child is almost grown, and I am astonished at how brief this era, almost past, has been. How brief my *life* has been. I am aware that the decades left to me will seem even briefer, so they had better be sweet. If I do not capture and celebrate what art I have, it will die. If I do not nourish myself, I will yearn for nourishment. If I do not connect myself with my own past in the things I do now, I will remain adrift from it. Those whom I have loved in the past cannot catch hold of me, for they are dead. It is I who must catch them.

My love works in the garden, pulling up maple saplings and planting roses. He comes inside, smelling like dirt and sweat and seeds, and he is all smiles from his digging in the earth. Coming down into the cool darkness of the basement, he finds me at my new machine. She has a free arm for cuffs and collars, a self-winding bobbin, fourteen different kinds of stitches, and a built-in buttonholer. She can sew with two needles at the same time. She is high-tech white, and most of her is plastic, the kind they use to make telephones. I can lift her with one hand.

I am working on a madras sundress for my granddaughter. I have cut it long so she can grow into it. I have a length of cotton for a dress for myself that I'll cut out when I finish Rosie's dress. One daughter sits on a heap of pillows in the corner, and we are talking quietly about nothing much. I come to the end of a seam, raise the needle, and automatically reach around to the back, where the presser bar lifter was on my grandmother's machine. I stop for a moment, missing her.

THE QUICK AND THE DEAD

WE ARE AT A CONFERENCE at a hotel in Philadelphia. As we register, we get the traditional welcome kit for conference participants: little odds and ends by which to remember the city. A key ring. A pen from Elverson National Bank. A where-to-eat-in-Philadelphia map. And a packet of Kleenex. At this annual conference, there are always facial tissues in the welcome kit. The participants all cry a lot.

It is the annual conference of The Compassionate Friends, an organization of people whose children have died. There are two thousand people here: mothers and fathers, brothers and sisters, grandparents. A sprinkling of clergy and others in the helping professions. I fit several of these categories. I am a priest. I am the mother of a dead child and the stepmother of another. I never knew the young man my husband misses so mightily. It wasn't until after he died that I met his dad. But I have dreamed of him. My own dead child never saw my face; he was too small to see, too small to cry, too small to live. But I saw *him*. Sixteen years later, I see him still. And in a dozen years of ordained ministry, I have watched at the bedsides and prayed at the gravesides of many young people. Too many. But then, even one would have been too many.

Outside the meeting room are the photo boards. I remember them from last time: six or eight free-standing bulletin boards, upon which people have thumbtacked their treasured photographs. Most are mounted on paper, and most have an accompanying written message.

> Our Doug,
> Always remembered, Always loved, Always missed.
>
> All our love,
> Mom, Dad, Betsy

The photographs and their legends are a magnet to us. As the conference proceeds, we return to them again and again. We stand before them, looking at the young faces look back at us with their hopeful eyes. Unlined faces, each full of a future that was not to be. Girls in cheerleading outfits and ballet costumes, boys in soccer uniforms, couples in prom clothes, babies in sweaters and bonnets. Big grins. Shy little smiles.

A lovely little girl smiles from two pictures on a cardboard mat. In one she waves tentatively from a carousel horse. In the other, she poses more formally, wearing a special dress and a bracelet and a ring. The message reads:

> Our precious little girl died of leukemia. She tried very bravely to live. We continue to try and live without her.

We search the young faces, we who once attended PTA meetings and basketball games. We read the brief attempts of other parents to sum up the unthinkable:

> Matthew
> Born July 24, 1964, in Knoxville, Tennessee
> Died July 6, 1987, in Richmond, Virginia
> Killed by a drunken driver
> College student, United States Marine, musician
> Pilot, kind and loving human being
>
> She was pursuing a career in nursing because she wanted to help people. She would have been excellent.
>
> He was impossible. He was delightful.
>
> Matt committed suicide.

or just

Kevin
17 years old
1968–1985

A mother points out her child's picture to another who stands beside her. Quietly, for the thousandth time, she recounts the story of the hospitalizations and the surgeries, using technical medical terms as she describes the cancer that savaged her only child. As her story breaks off in a sob, the other woman takes her hand without a word. They stand quietly for a long time, holding on to each other. Quiet tears trace familiar paths down their cheeks.

The discussion groups at the conference are breathtaking in the anguish they reveal. "Suicide." "Multiple Losses at Different Times." "Murder." "Only Children or All Children." "AIDS." Something for everyone in this buffet of pain and loss. But there is more: workshops aimed at finding meaning in the lives that remain after death has claimed a beloved child. "Dealing with Family." "What Can I Say to You?" "Telling the World How I Really Feel." Help in making life possible again. Although the two thousand people who have come here live with pain every day, the purpose of their fellowship is not simply to experience their pain. It is to support one another by sharing it, to find hope in the midst of suffering that seems unendurable but which must be endured.

At dinner we sit with a couple who lost their eighteen-year-old son less than a year ago. The wife is a tightly coiled spring of rage. The boy driving the car, she says, walked away without a scratch. He has never even said he was sorry. If she had a gun, she would kill him with great pleasure. She looks at me defiantly as she says this, as if daring me to temporize with her. Anger arcs from her like an electrical current. Her husband looks apologetically at my husband and changes the subject. How long has it been since your son died, he asks. Five years. The man looks at my husband and tries to imagine himself surviving five years of this. He can't. He asks if it gets any easier. It gets different, my husband answers. Not exactly easier. It's hard to explain.

I remember my own behavior when my third child was born too early to survive. How I paced the floor in the hospital late that night, as if I were looking for something. How I cried at home in my own bed the next night, and then never cried about it again. How proud I was of myself for getting back to normal so quickly, and of my husband of those days for doing the same. Does he ever remember, I wonder. I suppose he does. The marriage did not endure. Odd that it has not occurred to me until now that this loss and our stoic approach to it might have had something to do with that. An undeclared little life. An undeclared little death.

A waiter carries a tray of coffee cups down the hallway where the photographs are. He stops for a minute and studies them, moving from face to face, reading the messages of love and longing. I know that he is thinking what everyone here once thought: I could not survive if this happened to my child.

I think of the toy iron I saw in the Catacomb of Saint Callistus outside Rome. It was plastered between the stones in a catacomb wall, marking the tomb of a small girl. Her parents were too poor to afford an incised stone marking her tomb, and they placed the little iron there so they would be able to find her. They visited again and again, feeling along the cold stones until their fingers found the handle, and then they stood in the silent dark, touching the slab behind which their child lay. They remembered her, bustling along behind her mother, ironing with her little iron as the big iron glided back and forth in her mother's practiced hand. And then, one day . . . what? Something terrible happened. The toy iron, two thousand years old now, speaks silently of what her life and her death meant to the two people who loved her beyond all else. I remember the little iron as I stare at the pictures on the board. It is in little things that we know what it is to love a child, and so it is in little things that we feel what it is to lose one.

The facial tissues from my souvenir packet are all used up. I have used them to dry my own tears and the tears of other people here. I think I have even dried the two-thousand-year-old tears of the couple in the catacomb, coming from my own eyes. I don't begrudge a single one of those tears, my own or anyone else's. They are precious. They mark the spot, the important spot, a child held and still holds in our hearts, whether he was full of strength and wit like my husband's son or tiny and still like my own. We want to mark the spot where they lie. They deserve to be remembered by the world they left too soon.

A young man is pictured receiving a college diploma. Both he and the college president are beaming with happiness. He walks with two crutches, and has the barrel chest of someone who's been doing that all his life.

Born with spina bifida. He never gave up!
We are proud of his accomplishments.

I'll bet. I'm proud of him, and I didn't even know him. I walk and look, and I marvel at how brave ordinary people can be. Incredibly brave, both the dead and the living. To embrace a life that has ended too soon is brave. To experience the hurt through which such a life must be seen is brave. To be honest about loss and sorrow and terrible anger is brave. But through that bravery the children in the photographs live still. And always will.

♦

SNAKES OF THREE GENERATIONS

♦

"Rosie, don't move. Stand very still right where you are."

Even at four years old, Rosie knows enough to do what that tone of voice says. And she does stand stock still, her eyes wide. She and her mother, out on a walk, have been investigating a cat who seemed to be in trouble in some bushes. But he is not in trouble. He is trying to catch a snake, who is trying to writhe out of his clutches, and they are both thrashing around in the brush. The snake gets free, and darts out of the underbrush and across the road, its long body arcing this way and that in rapid *S*-curves. It is very strong and very fast. It slithers right in front of Rosie, who remains rooted to the pavement. It passes within a foot of her. Rosie and her mother watch as it zips across the road and disappears into the grass on the other side. Then Mommy opens her arms and Rosie runs to her. She does not cry. She is not afraid, not exactly. But she sees that her mother is shaken. And she remembers that voice—she has only heard it a few times in her life. It warns of a danger that has nothing to do with the clash of wills between mother and daughter, like other orders Rosie's mother gives her. That voice says nothing about whether Rosie has been good or bad. It commands absolute obedience in the name of survival. *Don't move. Stand very still right where you are.*

Her mother hates the snake because its expression does not change. It shows no emotion. It acts quickly to save its own life, like any other animal, but it acts inexorably, as if it were programmed. Not in fear, not running for its life, not lying in the grass afterward, panting, with its heart pounding in terror. She could pity an animal like that. She could want an animal who was more like us, who could be afraid like us, to escape. But the snake glides off and shows us no fear, gives us nothing to pity. Its eyes do not change, do not roll back in its head, showing their whites, do not show us large black pupils, pools of terror that are like ours. It faces death implacably, and does not acknowledge life with any show of feeling. And our blood runs cold. Something so indifferent to its own life must be hostile to ours. This makes no sense. Aren't most animals indifferent or hostile to people? But somehow we feel it more about snakes. They don't arch their backs so that we may pet them.

This snake was red and black. Was it bands of color or red on the underside, I ask on the phone when news of the snake sighting reaches me. We try to figure out what kind of snake it was. It doesn't sound like one I know. There aren't many poisonous snakes around here. None that I know of on the Jersey Shore. Copperheads like the woods better. Anyway, they're not red and black. I'll look it up. I used to look up snakes in the encyclopedia when I was a child, gazing at their fangs, their impassive faces, their expressionless eyes looking up at me from the page. I used to scare myself doing that. There was a picture of a man milking a rattlesnake, pressing its fangs against the edge of a beaker so the venom would drip inside. What if the snake twisted free? What if it sank those dripping fangs into the man's hand? What if it let itself fall from the table and slithered out the door of the laboratory and outside along the streets, and what if it found my house and it came there and I were playing in my yard and it came *there* and slid up behind me in the grass and buried its fangs deep into my leg? I wore boots sometimes when it wasn't raining because of that fantasy. Just in case.

Rosie's mother saw a snake when she was just about the same age. We were sitting out in the yard, her grandparents and I, while Corinna poked around, exploring. Suddenly she came running. "Mommy, there's a snake under the tree!" Her eyes were wide, too. We looked under the tree in a gingerly way, but the snake was gone. What did it look like, I asked. It was black. And it was eating a carrot. Are you sure about the carrot part? From that day forward we had a joke about the snake munching on a carrot, looking like Groucho with a cigar sticking out of the side of his mouth. About that snake eating the carrot, I'd say—are you sure you weren't making that up? To this day, she *knows* that the snake she saw when she was four was holding a carrot in its mouth. And I guess it was.

The snake eating a carrot was the first snake she remembered, but it wasn't actually her first snake. That snake was a pet, a garden snake named David who belonged to a friend. Corinna was less than a year old. Our friend handed her the snake. David bent himself into an *S* and stared fixedly at my baby as she held him in both chubby hands and laughed. David didn't smile. Take him back, I said, a bit sharply, she might hurt him. But I knew I wasn't really afraid of her hurting the snake. It was the other way around. I couldn't bear the sight of my baby holding that thing. I couldn't bear the way it writhed slowly in her hands. And the way it looked at her, its face expressionless, its eyes watching.

I am four. I am alone in our backyard. I am poking around in the vines that grow against the garage, looking for honeysuckle blossoms. My mother has just shown me how to find the drop of sweetness inside, and I want some. At my feet I see a shiny brown stick. I reach for it. It springs to life, bends away from my hand. In a moment, it is gone. I do not even see its head. I am frozen where I am for a few seconds. Then I run into the house to find my mother. I saw a snake outside, I tell her. I don't know if I am afraid or not. It is a garter snake, she says. It won't hurt you, but don't touch it.

If it won't hurt me, why shouldn't I touch it, I wondered.

There seemed to be something more that needed to be said here. But she need not have warned me off touching the snake. I was not disposed to touch the snake. A lifeless thing that suddenly moves, a thing that seems to be both animate and inanimate, that does not participate in the community of passion that I have already begun to perceive among the living: cats that cuddle and purr, dogs that lick your hand, cows that thrust their great heads at you so you can scratch between their horns, birds with broken wings that hop desperately in an effort to regain the air. I wanted to touch those animals. Some of them were more likely to hurt me than the garter snake. But I didn't want to touch him.

Medieval painters often represented the serpent in the Garden of Eden as a snake with a woman's head, thus marrying the almost-universal human dislike of snakes to the misogyny endorsed by the church of those days. Snakes are close to women, they hoped we would think, close to the rotting earth like women, with their bellies in the dirt. Sex is the problem, and women represented it. If the whole human race could just have been male, we'd have been fine.

I beg your pardon. Putting a woman's head on a snake's body does not hide what it is we fear, and what it is that the myth of the fall of our first parents attempted to explain: the presence of evil that is no respecter of persons. Whatever anxieties theologians may have attempted to instill in us, we are not really afraid of the powerful force that issues in the propagation of the race. As fascinated as the church has been with it for centuries, sex is *not* the problem. We fear something else: the steely gaze of death, the eyes that look at us without expression, the heart that does not beat faster even in fear for itself and hence will not beat faster in pity for us.

Sometimes you will find the empty skin of a snake on the side of a road. The snake has lain there, expanding and contracting its powerful muscles to work the skin loose, so the new skin it has grown underneath can be exposed. It tries to slide along rocks, or something else rough, so the old skin can get tattered enough to slip off. Finally it does, and the snake is free. The old skin lies there, an empty, snake-shaped bag. To lose its old skin is hard on the snake; it is exhausted by the process, and impelled through it by pain. But snakes do not show their pain as we do. They do not cry out. They are different from us. And so we do not pity the snake. We watch steadily and without emotion as it writhes against the rough stones, trying to get free. And our eyes do not change.

EGGS

"DON'T WORRY IF the people at Heuss House don't answer when you talk to them," I tell the girls. "Some of them are shy."

We are in the lobby of the skyscraper where Trinity Church's Girl Scout troop holds its meetings. Like scouts in more typical settings, the girls are supposed to do one service project a month. Today we will go to the John Heuss House, a drop-in center for the mentally ill homeless in lower Manhattan. It is Holy Saturday, the day before Easter. We're going to dye Easter eggs with the clients.

As we set out on our short walk, I congratulate myself on my delicate choice of words: to say that some of the people at Heuss House are shy is a major understatement. They are among the most fragile of this city's human beings, the ones people hurry past because they're talking to the air on the subway. Some of them don't talk at all, even to the air. Some have lived in their mental darkness since birth. Others had the sanity battered out of them afterward. Many are the deinstitutionalized mentally ill, released into the deadly custody of the streets.

Some Heuss House clients talk a lot. Shout, in fact. As we reach the door, I hope that nobody shouts at the girls while we're here.

Several tables have been set up, end to end, along one wall of the big common room. The familiar square boxes of Easter egg dye lie invitingly on them. Here are the eggs, we are told, and there they certainly are: two hundred hard-boiled eggs, filling the largest colander I've ever seen. The scout leaders and I exchange glances. Two hundred eggs.

Girl Scouts begin dyeing eggs, their heads bowed industriously over the bright colors in the bowls. Most of the clients ignore them, or look over with idle curiosity and then look away. I'll warm them up a little. I sit down with two men who have parked themselves and their belongings at a table.

"How're you guys doing?"

One smiles and says he's fine. The other says nothing.

"When was the last time you colored an Easter egg?"

"Oh, my," says my friend, "I believe it's been about thirty-five years."

"That's a long time."

At this the other man buries his head in his arms on the tabletop. I look at him. He appears to be asleep. His companion and I carry on.

"It sure is. Thirty-five years."

"You were just a little kid then."

"Yes, ma'am, I know that's the truth."

"How about doing one now?" I say. "We've got two hundred to do today."

"Two hundred?"

"Yessir."

"That's a lot of eggs."

"Yes, it is. Want to do a couple?"

"Well, maybe I will. In a few minutes."

So I get up and resume my table-hopping. I glance over at the scouts and am delighted to see Ramona, easily one of the center's most colorful clients, dyeing eggs and chattering away happily. Today Ramona is wearing a tight black-and-fuchsia bateau-neck top and toreador pants. Red nail polish and lipstick. Pink dangle earrings. The little girls don't appear to realize that Ramona is actually a young man.

Robin and Linda are the two scout leaders. We also have some mothers along to help, and a sprinkling of younger brothers and sisters. The women move quickly, filling more and more bowls with hot water and vinegar and dye tablets that instantly blossom red and blue and yellow and purple. They fill other bowls with more and more eggs, ready to go. The girls are each running two and three bowls apiece. So is Ramona, who is trying to create an egg that will match her nails. And now one of the men has joined in, pulling a chair up to the table and starting in on a yellow egg. He says to nobody in particular that it is for a special lady, and looks significantly at a female client, who looks away. Robin and Linda praise the eggs loudly, clients' and girls' alike. We talk a lot about how many eggs there are yet to be dyed. I peer into the colander. Looks like a good hundred fifty in there. I start another round of the tables.

One man says he dyed eggs last year with his brother's children. I wonder where his brother is now, and what the man is doing here. Person after person gives me his egg-dyeing vitae as I visit first one table and then another. They used to dye eggs at home. Or they never did. One man tells me he used to dye eggs for Allah and expects to do so again soon, at the end of all time. An exhausted-looking black woman tells me she has six children and doesn't know where they are right now. The children of most Heuss House clients are in foster care. Many of the younger clients grew up in foster homes themselves.

Chester has never colored an egg before. He is uncertain about sitting down with the girls, as he is uncertain about most things in his life. After some coaxing, he sits down. What color does he want? He is afraid to choose. I choose blue for him. It'll be like a robin's egg, I tell him. Chester looks anxious, and I realize he doesn't know about robins' eggs. A flash of memory: my grandmother on a summer morning, calling me out to the backyard to come and see. In her hand is the shell of a robin's egg, translucent blue. I look at Chester again and wonder about his grandmother. And his mother. Did somebody once look at his face and adore it? Did somebody want to show him beautiful things? Maybe not.

"Do I put it in there?"

"Yes, right in the bowl."

"My fingers'll get dirty."

"No, you use this wire dipper—see? Like this."

"Like this?"

"Yeah, that's right. That's good."

When one side of the egg is blue, Chester is uncertain about what to do next. He asks me how to make the other side blue. You turn it over, I say, like this. Chester has a hard time turning the egg, but eventually he does. He asks me when it will be done. When you like the way it looks, I tell him. He looks anxious again. Chester doesn't like choices. He asks permission to take it out of the dye. He starts another egg, checking each step of the procedure with me as he goes. He doesn't smile. He doesn't want to make a mistake.

Christina is sitting next to Chester. At nine, she is an experienced egg dyer and knows all the ropes. At the moment she is making a freehand egg, painting on different colors with a fingertip. The effect is lovely—sort of Matisse. Chester is watching. He looks at his own egg, sitting in its plain blue bath, and again at the Matisse.

"Can I make a rainbow egg?"

And tears sting my eyes. Uncertain, non-egg-dyeing, permission-asking Chester, who never had anybody help him learn much of anything when he was little, who grew up stunted, frightened of new things and also of old things: seized with the sudden conviction that he can create a

CANA LIBRARY
BERKLEY, MICHIGAN

thing of beauty. Robin and Linda are watching now. Christina matter-of-factly shows him the colors, and swirls a ribbon of orange around a virgin egg as an example. Chester does the same with a fresh one and holds it up to admire. He does the egg in three colors. And then he smiles.

◆ ORIGINAL SIN ◆

EVERYONE WHO HAS HAD CHILDREN knows about original sin. It's the thing we have in us that makes us think we're the center of everything. Theologians say that this is universal—no one escapes. They also throw in a few ideas about how it got that way, involving Adam and Eve and the snake and all the rest of it. Snake or no, parents know it's true. Children *do* think they're the center of the universe. And it's understandable that they do. When they are babies, if all goes well, they really do live in a world arranged around them and their needs. People stand over their cribs and watch them breathe. They cry and people try everything to make them stop: food, a nice, clean diaper, a satisfying burp, a cuddle. All that attention. It's as close to paradise as one gets in life.

I once witnessed the pivotal moment when that paradise ended for another human being. The being to whom this happened was my own daughter, with whom I had lived in harmonious partnership for eight months, she expressing a need and I filling it. Anticipating it, if I could. The days of her babyhood went dreamily by in this way, until one summer afternoon. I was sewing. I had spread the fabric out on the floor so I could pin the pattern pieces onto it. There were sharp pins and fragile pieces of tissue paper involved, so when my little one began to crawl over the cloth, I picked her up quickly and sat her down on the floor outside its perimeter. "*No!*" I said firmly. She sat there for a minute, absorbing the action and the word. Then she opened her mouth and howled.

I watched in awe. This was the first time she had experienced a limit. For the whole of her conscious life, I had been all smiles and applause at her all-fours explorations of the world. And now I was saying "no," and there was an exclamation point at the end of it, and I was stopping her from doing as she wished. This was the very first time it had ever occurred to her that her wish was not the final word to others that it was to her. It was an outrage.

And that is what it's like for all of us. We have all had that moment, whether or not there were witnesses. We think the world is ours, and then we learn that it is not. And it's an outrage. Sometimes I think that the whole of human error needs no fancier an explanation than this outraged response to that first "*No!*" Sometimes I think that all the lies in which people find themselves are nothing more than infuriated attempts to find a way around it.

It's often true of alcoholics, for instance, that they react violently to being told what to do. They'll drink themselves out of jobs and marriages and into comas rather than give in to pretty clear evidence that they're out of control, and they view statements to that effect on the part of those who live with them as extremely disloyal remarks. Often they'll explain their self-destruction in terms of their civil rights, or depict it as the only possible response to an impossible mate or a demanding job. The warm, sophisticated buzz of the first drink gives way to the soggy vertigo of the seventh or eighth, and still the drunk feels that he is in control.

Apparently there is a host of genetic and chemical reasons why he does this, but the words *he* chooses to explain it to himself and others are words about his own power: nobody is going to tell me what to do with my life. And until he can find some other words—what the people in recovery from addiction call "hitting bottom"—until he can admit that he has no power over alcohol, he does not change. He loses what power he does have in his insistence on claiming the power that is not his. And on the morning after a night like that, he looks at his haggard reflection in the mirror and lies. Sure, I drink too much, he says to himself. But I don't have a drinking *problem*. It doesn't really affect my life.

I remember a little boy—about two years old—who repeatedly refused a cookie he obviously wanted. "No," he said several times, gazing longingly at the sweet. His power to say "*No!*" to an adult meant more to him than his desire for the enjoyment of a treat, and he went without it. And I remember a woman who very much wanted to end a protracted quarrel with her husband, one that had had them in separate bedrooms for weeks. But she wouldn't end it. "I won't give him the satisfaction of knowing that I want him to move back into our room." And she did want him back. Not as much, though, as she wanted the power to say "no" to him. And not as much as she wanted to deny that he had any power over *her*.

The poet John Milton was fascinated with our willingness to do ourselves harm rather than surrender our power. He was fascinated with the mighty—and voluntary—plunge of Satan to dominion over the miseries of hell: "better to reign in hell than serve in heav'n" was how he put it, and we recognize the voice. That's the alcoholic speaking. Or the little boy who would rather say "no" than enjoy a sweet. Or the woman who would rather sleep alone than show her need. I'd rather be queen of my own pain than submit to the power of another to heal it. Milton, of course, was blind when he wrote *Paradise Lost*. He could not transcribe his own poems. He had to dictate them to one of his daughters. He could not walk outside his house alone. Someone had to lead him. He had learned, in an especially painful way, what it was to be powerless. But he had also learned what it was *not*. It is not powerless to be limited. Limits are part of life. Some limits are profound. Blindness is one. There are others. But having limits is not the same thing as powerlessness. And the unchallenged exercise of the will is not necessarily power. It can be terrible bondage.

The year of my daughter's run-in with original sin was 1969. She wasn't the only person that year who was outraged at limits. People a lot older than eight months felt exactly the same as she did. In a way that the healthy-minded citizenry of the 1990s finds hard to follow, the dictates of one's impulses and desires carried a moral freight that was pretty absolute. It was not just pleasing to do one's own thing. It was good for the world. It seemed at the time to be part of the fabric of the universal struggle against oppression. Oppression of the poor by the rich, of the East by the West, of the black by the white, of the woman by the man. The overthrow of self-control was a part of this struggle. In those days, before everybody famous had either died of drug overdoses or founded rehabilitation clinics, the use of mind-altering substances was an important—if tacit—statement of personal alliance with the worldwide movement toward liberation. So was the resolute avoidance of a commitment to sexual fidelity. So was a contempt for the business world. Nothing in American society would occasion greater amazement to a time traveler from the 1960s than the idea that one day there would be a *drug problem* on *Wall Street*. One of the reasons he used drugs was that the establishment did not. And he would have difficulty with the term "drug problem." It's no problem, man.

Nothing was more important than freedom. That was morally clear in the case of the visibly oppressed—the Vietnamese, the farm workers. And the children of privilege in the West, lacking more sinister oppressors they could call their own, fought the limits placed on them by life. Not knowing what we now know about the poison of drugs and the worse poison of their deployment among the poor, not knowing, yet, about the virus that was even then planting its invisible ensigns in some of their bloodstreams, they smashed the protective barriers of interpersonal duty and duty to self and, in smashing them, felt brave. Although I was preoccupied with motherhood at the time, and could do little more than hum along, I do remember viewing what later could only be called self-destructive acting-out through an admiring lens that made it look like gallant iconoclasm.

Freedom was understood to be *from* restraint. It was freedom *from*, not freedom *to*. Freedom to what? It wasn't always very clear. And when the cost of that freedom began to be apparent, when people began to go crazy and die from doing drugs, when people owned up to the loneliness of their rootlessness and promiscuity, the political scaffolding that supported that behavior—that which had made it possible to see it as something brave—collapsed. And never arose. You would have a hard time finding someone today who would argue that drugs are a way to a higher consciousness that could transform the world. Or that self-knowledge and self-love are enhanced by sleeping with a lot of different people. But many people thought so then.

I guess the culture of the sixties hit bottom, as the people in recovery would say. We became people who could discriminate between limits that were repressive and limits that were necessary. I guess we learned that encountering a "*No!*" doesn't wipe a person out. My daughter's world *did* end the day I gave her that shock, but she set about building another world, one more consonant with the way things are. I see rock singers from the sixties on the television today, talking about their sobriety with the earnestness of people who have almost died. Gifted people, some of them. In those days they would have told you that their giftedness was the result of their being completely free to be what they wanted to be. Now they talk about their Higher Power. And about surrender. And about confession and restitution. They are heavier, their faces lined and middle-aged. They have a lot less hair. And a lot more peace.

The world doesn't seem to work well when we are at the center of it. People can be practically dead and still think that everything is fine. Being made to move from that place feels like an outrage. Like being cast out of the Garden of Eden. But you can't be happy until you leave. *Felix culpa*, the medieval theologians called it. It means "fortunate fall."

WORKING THE WATERFRONT

THE MOTOR VESSEL *Alchatby* was sailing in the evening from Red Hook Terminal in Brooklyn. She would go thence to Norfolk, then to Charleston, and then she would head out across the Atlantic to her home port of Alexandria. In two months—more if the weather is bad—she would return to New York to take on cargo again, and the loop would be repeated: New York, Norfolk, Charleston, Alexandria, over and over again.

The port chaplain climbed up the gangway on her maiden visit to the *Alchatby*, laden with pamphlets and subway maps and *National Geographic*s older than the mess boy. The crew was hanging over the railing and looking out the portholes, pointing at me and digging each other in the ribs and laughing. I made it to the top and gasped, "*Mar-ha-ban.* Seamen's Church." A murmur of recognition went through this Moslem crowd at the words "Seamen's Church," for we are known to seafarers of all nations and faiths. And the crowd moved inside, through the greasy passage into the crew's lounge, where they descended upon the magazines like locusts.

"How are things on your ship?" I asked, and they answered "No problem," the foreign seafarer's stock answer to any question put to him in English. "Where is the seamen's club from here?" "How can we get there?" "Can we telephone Egypt?" "Can you change a hundred dollar bill?" "I want to buy some blue jeans." We talked about our families and showed each other pictures. I received two offers of marriage for my daughter, who was beautiful and the perfect age, being fifteen at the time. But then Mahmoud, the steward, melted into the room and, with a beatific smile, ended it all by announcing, "The captain sees you now." I followed him up the ladder to captain country. The captain was there with two officers. At a wave of his hand, they were gone.

As ships go, this one was modest. I told the captain it was very fine and he agreed. He presented me with a package of Dunhill cigarettes and one of Cleopatras, the cigarette of Egypt—the packet was gold with a picture of

Cleopatra and, I think, her autograph in a cartouche on the front. "Cleopatras are the best cigarette in the world," he said, lighting up a Dunhill and offering me one. Mahmoud, who seemed to respond by telepathy to the captain's unspoken wishes, reappeared this time with an enormous tray full of food, and it was spread before us: boiled eggs, eggplant fried in sesame oil, tiny meatballs on a bed of chopped sautéed leeks, pita bread, cubes of cheese, caviar, shrimp in a yoghurt sauce. This was not dinner, the captain said, it was just a snack. We ate and talked, I explaining our services and he asking questions and telling me about his life. I saw that he was a lonely man, this captain. His wife was dead and his children were in Egypt, cared for by servants while he sailed the seas. He was worried about his daughter, afraid that she wouldn't find the proper husband without him there to monitor her choice. He had fought under Sadat and hoped never to fight again. When he heard that Sadat had been killed, he cried. Throughout our discussion we continued to eat. When I had stuffed myself just short of physical pain, Mahmoud was suddenly there. He and the captain surveyed the remaining food—easily enough for another three or four people—and exchanged a mournful glance. "You do not like our food," the captain said sadly. I hastened to assure him that he was wrong, that it was the best in the world, and he happily agreed. It turned out that the captain was an expert marksman and had rigged up a makeshift pistol range for himself, so we closed the visit out on the deck with a few minutes of target practice. He scored higher than I did, which seemed right to him. And he took me to the gangway himself, pressing another pack of Cleopatras into my hand.

It was still dark when the *Pioneer* glided into its berth along the dock in Port Elizabeth. The deck crew shivered in the early morning cold, waiting to toss the ropes to the longshoremen waiting below. Soon the metal gangway was lowered into place. As the sun came up, visitors came and went: customs inspectors, immigration officials, shipping agents, longshoremen, checking the ship's cargo and its crew, conferring with the deck officer about where the unloading process would begin. In no time at all the giant cranes were in place and running, and forty-ton containers swung up and off the ship, suspended sixty feet in the air from slender cables. The noise was deafening: horns blowing to warn of an approaching straddle-carrier, truck engines running, containers crashing onto trailers, men shouting and swearing at one another as they went about their business.

I was on the dock, pawing through the trunk of my car to see if I had any Bibles written in Urdu with me. I remembered that a man on this ship had wanted one last time and I hadn't had any. Today I did; I scooped it up, along with some subway maps and some 1978 *National Geographic*s and began the climb up the gangway. I was met by the watchman, and together we edged past a longshoreman who was blocking the door and entered the ship. We made our way along the corridor until we reached the messroom, where the cook was sitting, sleepily smoking a cigarette. I knew him from other visits to this ship, and so we had a cup of tea together and chatted. Things were okay on board, he said; the voyage up from South America was rough this trip, and everybody had been working since two this morning to come alongside. Nobody was sick or injured. This cook always knows how people are on board. He is sort of like the mother. He looked longingly at the *National Geographic*s, and so I let him have first crack at them. Just make sure you share them when you're finished, I said. He laughed, and said he would if they didn't complain too much about the food. He padded off into the galley to start the soup for lunch, the magazines tucked protectively under one arm.

Things were much busier in the captain's office. All morning, he had entertained a stream of ship's chandlers, agents, longshoremen, and customs inspectors. He looked up wearily as I entered and broke into a smile: he knew I didn't want him to sign anything, buy anything, explain anything, or decide anything. He was Yugoslavian, as were his senior officers, and he commanded a crew of thirty-six Yugoslavs and Pakistanis who didn't always understand one another very well. Like the cook, the captain thought things on board were going pretty well: not as much cargo as anyone would like, but more than last voyage. I told him he looked tired, and he shook his head and sighed. A poster showing a picture of Dubrovnik was taped to the wall. Beside it was a photograph of a pretty, dark-haired woman and two small children. There was a calendar there, too, with the days crossed off in red and the day of his homecoming circled. How many more days, I asked, and he was able to tell me exactly. A Pakistani steward and the Yugoslav radio officer were the only people on board who were able to come back to the seafarers' center with me. They wanted to telephone their families at home. As we entered, the lunchtime crowd of truckers and longshoremen was beginning to filter in, and soon the place was full of people and the smell of hamburgers cooking and the sound of the jukebox. The Platters were doing "The Great Pretender." The pinball machines blinked and rang; men kicked them and swore at them while other men stood and watched, criticizing their technique. It was a cheerful world of dungarees and workboots, grimy hands and loud conversations.

The port of Newark-Elizabeth is, by some counts, the largest container seaport in the world. It is the hub of the shipping industry in the Atlantic, and a loading center for a new generation of giant container ships that circumnavigate the globe. Its population on a given working day is more than twenty thousand, including seafarers, longshoremen, truckers, merchants, ship chandlers, and anyone else whose business takes him into the world of shipping. At night, by contrast, it is almost empty except for the ships sitting silently in the water and the police cars cruising the deserted streets. It is at night that the seafarers are free to come to the club and get some of the things they need: A phone call home to see if everyone is all right in Korea or El Salvador or India or Greece. A game of Ping-Pong or pool. A worship service in a language they understand. An hour's quiet conversation with a chaplain who knows something about the loneliness of their lives. There is a little store in the club. It sells razor blades and toothpaste and garish little plates that say "New York" on them. Postcards showing the Manhattan skyline. Souvenirs of New York, the city the seafarers have heard about all their lives. Most of them will not get any closer to it than this club, which is not in New York at all. It is in New Jersey. Turnaround time is fast. The ships are in and out of the port in twelve hours.

Christmas Eve. It was cold, and the water was dark black as I drove past the deep, still Newark channel, past the ships sitting alongside with their lights blazing in the cold, past the memorial to dead longshoremen, past the Catholic chapel where Father Charlie was getting ready for mass. I pulled into our parking lot. The door to the seafarers' center had iced shut again; after a brief fight, I pried it open and turned on the lights.

We had decorated the club with wreaths, and an artificial Christmas tree had been up since just after Thanksgiving. As many red poinsettias as we could afford were banked in front of the altar in the chapel. Other people were starting to arrive now, carrying cakes and plates of food and Christmas presents for the seafarers. Joe the van driver arrived and began his rounds, picking up people from the ships and bringing them in for Christmas Eve. A man whom I suspected of selling hot merchandise in the port turned up with two enormous bags of gifts for the seafarers to take home to their children: dolls, small purses, toy trucks. I commended the good deed, and he left happily. I arranged the things he had brought under the tree and added our own to the pile. We delivered ten thousand handmade sweaters and caps and scarves and socks to the ships in the weeks just before Christmas. I kept fifty of them hidden away for tonight.

Father Charlie's mass was finished, and he arrived with

a group he had brought over from his place, carrying still more presents. Joe dropped off vanload after vanload of seafarers, and they milled around the center with the chaplains and the volunteers. There were also a cop and a few port workers who had to work on Christmas Eve.

We did the worship service in different languages, all at the same time. Sometimes we took turns, switching from Korean to English to Chinese to Tagalog and back to English. Sometimes we all spoke at once, each in his own language, producing a pleasant hum of syllables and ending in unison with a great "*Amen!*" The seafarers followed along, joining in where they could, and we closed the service with "Silent Night." So quiet. Men's eyes filled as they thought of their homes. In the Philippines, it was already Christmas morning.

There was no point in making people feel miserable when they're away from home and couldn't do a thing about it. We put some music on the record player and began enjoying the food people had brought. One of the women volunteers danced with a young man from Honduras, and two Korean seafarers danced together, laughing uproariously at themselves. Seafarers lined up at the phones, and you could hear them shout when they got through: "Maria? Hello! Maria? *Feliz Navidad!*" The seafarers chose their presents from under the tree; I encouraged them to take more than one toy if there was more than one child at home. They were hesitant at first, but soon their arms were full.

The *Lloyd Bermuda* was in tonight. This was unexpected. Ordinarily she would have left already on her weekly New York–to–Bermuda run, but an accident in the yard slowed down the loading and so the men of the *Lloyd* were here on Christmas Eve. The *Lloyd* was a tiny ship. For eight years she had made the same run, and the eleven men on board had come in to the club every week. Most of them had been with her for much of those eight years; a few were new. An American captain rotated on and off command with a German captain. This voyage it was the American captain's turn. They were very lucky, the cook told me. They didn't think they'd be able to come to the party.

A young man from the *Lloyd* wheedled me into opening the store. He wanted to buy a watch for his girlfriend in Bermuda. I showed him the four Timex watches that were left, and he selected a pretty one with a gold band. Then he talked me into wrapping it for him. I told him he should stop going to sea and become a salesman, that I thought he had a future. He laughed.

It was time to go. Joe rounded everybody up and began returning them to their ships. Handshakes and Christmas wishes and addresses were exchanged. We cleaned up the mess and headed home.

Three days later I was listening to the radio as I fell asleep. On the news it said that a ship was in trouble off the Atlantic coast. There was a terrible storm. The last message from the captain was that there were twenty-foot seas and they were preparing to abandon ship. The ship was the *Lloyd Bermuda*. I got up and called the Coast Guard to see if I could get some inside news. They transferred me up to the Woods Hole command, which was managing the rescue. They were out looking for the *Lloyd* now. The storm was still raging and the temperature was in the teens, hampering the rescue effort. Did I know the color of the lifeboats on the *Lloyd,* by any chance? Did I know if the men had survival suits? I cursed my memory: I'd been on that ship a hundred times, but I couldn't remember the color of the lifeboats. I thought they were orange. But I didn't know. And I didn't know about the suits.

The storm continued for hours. They found one man. His arm was broken, but he had lashed himself to a piece of wood and he was alive. Then they found three more. One slipped out of his lifejacket as they were pulling him out of the water and disappeared beneath the icy sea. Another was found and died before they could get him to a hospital. Three alive. Two dead. That left six unaccounted for.

The house was dark and still. Everyone else was asleep. I sat there by the phone, thinking about Christmas Eve. About how the cook had said they were lucky to have been delayed so they could go to the party. About the kid who bought the watch. About the sweaters and scarves we gave them to keep them warm.

MY MOTHER AND I HAVE GOTTEN ALONG REALLY WELL SINCE SHE DIED

MY MOTHER WAS SORT OF A SAINT. She was a person whom everybody loved. Even crabby people, people whom nobody else could stand, always got a sympathetic hearing from her. This was especially true at the end of her life, when she was in bed much of the time and had no ready means of escape. But her welcome to them was genuine, as it was to everyone, the sunny and the glum alike. She wanted to think the best of people, and so she did. They appreciated it. When she died, the world became a grimmer place.

It wasn't always easy being the daughter of someone that nice, though. It was almost impossible, for instance, to tell her something negative. I was unable, at fifteen, to be completely forthcoming to a question about sex phrased this way: "You and Gene are . . . morally right with each other, aren't you?" I don't know whether I longed to confess that we were already pretty far south of what I knew she meant by "morally right" or not. I probably didn't. But I do know that I couldn't have answered no to that question. I mumbled something that I hoped sounded vaguely affirmative, and she changed the subject.

She was good. Really good. And because she was so good, she really didn't want to know about bad things. She would go to extraordinary lengths not to know about them. When my youngest child was two, she suffered a terrible injury to her left eye, one that would result in permanent blindness. In the fearful hours following the accident, as we sat through the emergency surgery and the anguish of our toddler's postoperative terror and confusion, not knowing if she would retain her eye at all, much less her sight, I took a minute to call my mother from the nurses' station. Quietly I filled her in on the gravity of the situation and the doubtful prognosis. I will never forget her response. With desperate cheer, she said, "Everything will be all right. Everything is always all right, isn't it?" There was a note of pleading in her voice.

Well, no, Mom, I can't rightly say that everything is always all right. I was angered by that telephone call, even though I knew that she wasn't able to do anything else. I was angered at being asked to say that things were okay when they weren't. I would have felt more supported, I think, by silence than I felt by that desperate plea for affirmation of a worldview that had a few pieces missing. But that was my mother. I think she was afraid that the admission of the smallest of negatives would precipitate an avalanche of despair. So she never let one in.

As she neared the end of her life, increasingly debilitated by heart disease, I tried once to have a talk with her about death. She was visiting me in my home, and she lay resting on the couch. I sat on the floor next to her, and she held me in her arms. I rested my head on her chest—ever so lightly, for she had a terrible scar there from heart surgery, and it was always tender. I told her that I was sad and afraid when I thought about the possibility that she might die. I told her that I loved her. After I had said these things, she answered. With her *voice*, of course, she told me that she was sure everything would be all right because she had such good doctors! But her hands stroking my hair, the smell of her, her arms and her soft skin told me what she could not say: that she loved me, too, and that that love would prove stronger than anything that could happen to her wasting body. Her words were the same relentlessly cheery things she'd been saying all her life. But a powerful truth was told in that moment in which I expressed my fears and she denied them. Something in her body acknowledged the things she couldn't say. And, although she was never able to speak the sad truth about herself, I felt that we had said what was needed. I felt I had cracked the code of her desperate cheer, accepting the ways in which she could tell the truth and the ways in which she couldn't.

People of my generation are most anxious that talk

about feelings be explicit. Men gather in groups and cry and write books about how their fathers never said "I love you" to them. It is a truism of our age that nothing should ever be inferred: everything needs to be spoken clearly and named. And I've no doubt that things should be named. I get as frustrated as the next person when I have to fill in the blanks for myself. But sometimes I wonder if our absorption in the ways in which our parents did not say things might not blind us to the ways in which they did say them. We have been shrill in our demands that they speak our language. Mightn't we bestir ourselves a bit and try to understand theirs? And don't we regard our own aggressive frankness with too admiring an eye sometimes? I know many people who talk a great deal about love and demonstrate very little. I'm not at all sure the strong, silent type wouldn't be preferable. And, with all my mother's inability to speak about her fears or about mine, I could read them through the screen of her bright small talk. We are very clear today about the need to be courageous and honest about expressing our negative feelings. My mother didn't do that very well. She was often afraid to say that she was worried, as if saying it would make something bad happen. So she was awfully cheerful, like Fred and Ginger dancing across the screen while the Depression ached on and on. No, it wasn't totally honest. But it enabled her to be brave in her own way. She used to drive me nuts sometimes, with her desperate cheer. But it wasn't so hard to see what lay behind it. And now, of course, it's very easy.

My second child was born at 4:35 on a Wednesday afternoon. At 4:42 the phone rang in the delivery room. It was Mom.

"How are you?" she asked brightly.

"Well, I'm pretty tired," I said. How the heck had she gotten through, I wondered. Delivery rooms were not the relaxed, homey places then that they are today. The doctor was just tying off the episiotomy.

"Well?"

"Well, what?"

"Well, how *are* you?"

"Well, I just had a baby five minutes ago, so I'm tired. You know how it is."

"Is it a boy or a girl?"

"It's a girl."

"A girl! What does she look like?"

"Round. She's kind of purple right now."

The doctor and the nurse were looking at each other over their masks. I guess they didn't get many calls back there. My mother said a few more things about not being able to believe she had gotten me right there in the delivery room and I told her I couldn't believe it, either. It was something, all right. I told her I had to go and we said good-bye.

"How'd she get through back here?" the doctor asked.

"I don't know. I guess she just asked nicely." That was certainly it. She was so nice that nobody stopped her. And so nice to me, too, in her vague inquiries about my health. I thought of how long she must have had to sit on her hands to keep from calling. This pregnancy had been difficult and dangerous. My baby had almost died, and pretty much all I had been able to do for months was to lie in bed and hope that she wouldn't. How absurd and perfect it was that my mother telephoned me in the delivery room at its successful conclusion to inquire politely how I was. It was pure Mom.

I received another call from her on the morning she was to die. She had been in the hospital for a long time, mortally weakened, we all knew, by congestive heart failure. A machine rotated tourniquets on all of her extremities, so that what was left of her circulation wouldn't have so many places to go all at once. She was nauseated most of the time, and had a hard time breathing. And a harder time speaking. But that morning she called. In a voice I had never heard before, a thin, wild voice, full of effort as she forced the words out, she told me that we shouldn't come that day. Everything would be all right, and we really shouldn't come all that way.

I muttered something noncommittal and told her to get some rest. I knew that she knew she was dying and didn't want us to see it. I wish she hadn't wanted to spare us that way, but of course she did. Dying is such a direct thing to do. She knew that her cheerfulness could no longer conceal the fact that it was happening. She felt a bit rude, and a bit of a bother. And so she hoped to slip away unnoticed so that no one would be sad.

My brother and I went, of course. And were able to say good-bye. As we stood over her and watched her struggle for each breath, I leaned over and whispered in her ear that everything was all right and she didn't need to fight anymore if she didn't want to. And everything was all right. Just as she had always said it was.

♦

THE NEW MATH

♦

BEING AN ADULT IS BETTER THAN being a kid. You no longer have to do as many things you're not good at as you did when they were still trying to make you well rounded. So—if you are lucky—you have by now found out where your strengths are and you have put yourself in a position of being able to call upon those skills frequently. You have also found out where your weaknesses are and—again, if you are lucky—you have found a way to make sure that they are not central to your job. Most of us know we're good at something, and we find a way to do that something *a lot*, and so we feel pretty decent about ourselves.

But there are a number of adults who are in some doubt about their abilities: those people who have tried to help their junior high school children with their math homework. "Can you help me with this?" asks your child. "Sure," you say, and you sit down. You get a clean sheet of paper and you have your child put his name on it. And the date. Then you ask him to copy the problem on the first line. He does. You're ready to go.

The page in the book you're working from doesn't look much like any page in the math books you remember from your own youth. You look at the sample problem in the book that, the teacher has told your child, has very clear explanations. The book says that the lowest common denominator (LCD) can easily be found using the least common multiple (LCM), and it suggests that you use prime factor form to find this. Remember to use each factor to its highest power, it says, not like finding the greatest common factor (GCF), where you would want to use the lowest power of each factor common to both numbers.

Okay. You look at the problem again. "You should never do math with a pen," you tell your child, and go off to find a pencil in the drawer. You recopy the problem in pencil. You remember that you knew how to do this when you were twelve. You think you remember how to begin, and you make make an × in between the two fractions. You're going to cross-multiply, you say to your child, to get them both in the same terms, and then you'll go from there. What is cross-multiply, your child asks. He says the teacher told them to do it a different way. You erase the ×. You draw a line under the problem on the page. A single numeral shines at the bottom of the page. This is the answer. Why do they have the answer there, you ask your child. The important thing is that you use the right method, he says, not whether you get the right answer. Oh.

Your child picks up the pencil and writes down the next step. He understands this part, he says. It's the next step he doesn't get. You look at what he has done and realize that you don't know what it means. You look at the book so that you can read the very clear explanation of this step, and it refers you to the previous page. You turn backward, and read the explanation. It sounds a little sarcastic. It uses initials you do not recognize to explain the first step. You read it again to see if you can figure out what the initials mean. They do not ring a bell. You turn back to the problem and stare hard at it. You take the pencil from your child and draw another line under the original problem. You press down hard on the pencil. Didn't his teacher explain this to him in class, you ask in a voice that has an accusing edge to it. I understood it then, he says in a trembly way, but I can't do it now.

You work on, searching the very clear explanations for clues. The numeral at the bottom of the page has a mocking look to it now. Your voice is tight, your sentences curt when you speak to your child, who grows quieter and quieter. His misery is palpable. You know that he is wishing he hadn't asked you for help. By the time you give up, you wish you were dead. You have failed to understand and execute a math problem that is intended to be understood and executed by people whose voices haven't changed yet and who are too young to drive a car. Not only have you failed to execute the problem, you cannot even understand enough to begin. Not even to *begin.* You are furious at the book and furious at the teacher, and you say to yourself that anyone who would voluntarily teach this stuff is a geek with no life. You do not *value* math. The only people who are good at it are losers with no people skills. You have people skills, you remind yourself. Right. That's why you want to kill a math teacher you've never met, because you're so good with people.

Math is very important. Your child knows a kid who wins prizes in math, goes to science fairs with an exhibit he made about an equation. Your child has five more years after this one before he goes to college, and math is very important in getting into college. Next year is going to be harder than this year. Certainly. And then there will be the next year, and the next, and then the next two years. And you are utterly without a glimmer of an idea about what is going on in the math book *this* year. You realize that you are going to be of no help to him in math for the rest of his life. He will get a 3 on the SAT. Doors will slam shut. He'll be fifty-five and still living at home.

There is nothing that stings like being unable to do something you know you should be able to do. In a matter of minutes the feeling of failure poisons your self-worth, which is why most of us set up our lives so that we can avoid those things that we don't do well. And why a kid is such a hard thing to be. Maybe I'll never be anything, he thinks. I can't do this. Math is important.

Well, yes, it is. And all kinds of things are possible for us as a culture because some people are so good at it.

And they're probably *not* all losers and geeks. I made that up. They probably have people skills, too.

You mellow out a little, thinking these things. You remember that you are an adult, and that you make your living in a job that doesn't use math. You balance your checkbook and do your taxes, period. It's enough. You remember your child slumped in his chair next to yours, remember the tears in his voice as you accused him of not being good at something you are not good at. You regret that. You reach out and stroke his hair. Can you call someone who can help? He shakes his head, blinking back tears. Then let's put this away and try later. Or let's ask the teacher for some extra help.

And you tell him you are sorry you were so mean. That you were really mad at yourself. Then what did you yell at me for, he asks. And you tell him again that you are sorry.

ADA GOES HOME

ADA STOOD ALONE at the church coffee hour, silent and erect. She was dressed in red from head to toe: a turban of her own fashioning wrapped around her hair, a red sweatshirt over a red turtleneck with a red skirt and red trousers tucked into her socks. Without any effort, she created a space around herself, and no one invaded it. People were helping themselves to coffee and slices of pound cake, catching up on each other's weeks. Ada held a Styrofoam cup of coffee in her hand.

I was working the room, shaking

hands with people in my new congregation and learning their names, when I found myself face-to-face with Ada. I was awed by her costume and by the moat she created around herself. She crossed it first.

"Are you the new reverend?"

"Yes, Barbara Crafton's my name. And you are . . . ?" I offered my hand and she shook it. The fingers on her proffered hand were intricately bandaged, I noticed, with a combination of gauze and a rubber band woven through them.

"I'm Ada. I've been a member of this church for a long time." She smiled, revealing a front tooth outlined in gold.

I was glad to hear it. A church that could claim both Alexander Hamilton and Ada as members seemed to me to be a community of some breadth. Looking at the other women's understated clothing and Ada's fearsome attire, though, I wondered what the experience of being a member of Trinity Church meant to her. Did she have friends here? I watched her stillness in the crowd and the way she cherished her coffee as she stared straight ahead.

Most days I would see her in the back of Trinity Church in the afternoon. Or in Saint Paul's Chapel, always at the back, walking back and forth near the door. Or at the coffee hour, carefully dressed in her incredible rags, her head wrapped tightly, her leggings tucked into heavy socks, a skirt over the leggings in the style adopted by homeless women. It is easier to wear a garment than it is to carry it. One day, one of her eyes was bloody.

"Ada, what happened to you?"

"I got hit."

"That's terrible. Does it hurt now?"

I knew better than to ask her how she happened to get hit. Or who had done it. If she wanted me to know, she would tell me. But it turned out that today was a day for talking. She smiled, her gold tooth a quick gleam, and began to hold forth. Not about the blow that had bloodied her eye, but about the way people don't do the right thing, about the way they don't leave other people alone, about the way men, especially, don't leave people alone. And who was she, Ada wanted to know, that men should bother her?

"I am no*body*. Why does anybody want to be messin' with me? I am no*body*. I am fifty years old. I got three children. I got nothin' for nobody. What they want to be poking at me for?"

It frequently seems to Ada that men are after her. One day she had to be taken from the church, screaming. One of the vergers had designs on her. The man in question, mild-mannered and happily married, was startled to learn that he was the culprit. All he had done was ask her to move to a different pew. Another time it was a prominent vestry member. Always men of color. Ada herself is black. Her ideal man is Jack Moody, one of the priests at Trinity. She drops his name as if he were a movie star. Jack is white.

"Only Rev'rend Moody. That's the only man I'll talk to. Most men, they make my side hurt." She puts a hand to her waist. "It hurts me when they come pushin' at me. Right here. They come pushin' on me, and my side hurt so bad!" She attends most of the noon masses, always by herself in the pew, standing regally erect in her monochromatic outfits. When it comes time to exchange the peace she greets her neighbors with a dazzling smile if they are women, and not at all if they are men. When it comes time to receive the Communion wafer she smiles again and looks me straight in the eye.

Ada has three children. They're all grown. One of them, the middle one, is crippled. Cerebral palsy, Ada says. He's up in Poughkeepsie. With whom, I wonder. With a lady up there, she says when I inquire. Oh. How long did Ida care for her own children? Was she always as she is now? It seems that she was not. She did some traveling; two children were born in New York, but one, the middle boy, was born in Alabama. Where Ada herself was born. She must have gone home to have that baby.

Ada sits in the chair beside my desk. "My family is so bad," she says. "You can't believe how bad they are. That's why I never did no drugs. I never drank no liquor. I grew up with that."

Ada's grandmother in Alabama used to send her to the store to buy whiskey. Ada was eight. Ada's father was a farmer. I don't know anything about a mother. She learned a lot about the Bible from someone, and reels off scripture verses lickety-split when she gets going. One of Ada's sisters is married. She and Ada never got along. Ada herself never got married. She tells a story about her man and the way she found out he had another woman. The story is a little different each time she tells it. She giggles like a schoolgirl when she talks about marriage and men. She wants me to guess which man in the church is interested in her. I can't guess. "I'll tell you tomorrow," she says, and giggles, a girlish giggle that starts out low and ends up high and lasts too long.

Ada sleeps on the ferry as it goes back and forth between Battery Park and Staten Island. The maintenance people on the ferry sometimes give her and the other women who ride the ferry at night money to clean the restrooms while they take a break. Ada believes that she is accorded this privilege more often than the other women because of the way she dresses. "They give me the job first because I got my head wrapped. Those other women, they say, 'Ada, why you get that job like that every day?' They think I got something. I ain't got nothin'." Ada buys her clothes in thrift shops. She spends $10 or $20 a month, out of an income of $465, on her outfits. It is clear that she puts a great deal of thought into them. "You've got style, Ada," Jack Moody always says to her, and she giggles.

There are times when Ada's personal demons get the better of her. Sometimes there is a grim, wild look in her eyes, and she talks rapidly and steadily about unnamed evil people. She barely pauses for breath. She quotes vengeful scripture to buttress her obscure points, and cannot be deflected from her soliloquy. Other times she barely speaks at all. She is tired, her face gray from a night on the ferry with no sleep. She is scarcely able to keep her eyes open as she struggles to talk to me.

I find a bed for Ada at a shelter for homeless women on 40th Street. It is run by sisters of several different Roman Catholic orders. It is clean and pleasant there, with a cheerful dining room and a quiet chapel. The dormitories are quiet, too, and a crucifix hangs on each wall. I give Ada a subway token and tell her how to get there. She is interviewed and accepted. That night I think of her snuggling down under the covers of her very own bed. The sisters say she can stay there for a while.

But a few days later our secretary comes in with the news that she saw Ada running down the street as if the devil himself were after her. I wait to hear what happened. The sisters call. They had asked Ada to undergo a psychiatric examination, as all their guests are asked to do. She bolted. "It's not unusual," Sister Nancy sighs. "Anyway, she was a little disruptive on the floor. She would cry in her sleep at night and wake the other ladies."

Ada's own explanation for leaving the sisters is a bit different. "They don't have God in their heart," she explains. "You have to come in at five-thirty. Not before. I can't stay there no more. I can't be in that pressure from those rules they have. I can't be in no pressure. They have evil in their hearts, and it makes pressure on me."

Win Peacock says that Ada is one of the most chronically homeless clients he has. Win runs John Heuss House, a drop-in center for the mentally ill homeless. Ada goes there sometimes. Win's known Ada for about eight years. "If she'd see our psychiatrist and take some medication, she could control herself better. But she won't do that. And we can't make her."

It's true. Ada won't see the nurse who comes regularly to Heuss House. She'll only see Win, who's right up there with Jack Moody as one of the few men she trusts. "Why don't you go down to Beaver Street?" I say. That's what Ada calls Heuss House: Beaver Street. "They're getting ready to have dinner over there. You could have a bite." Sometimes she does. Sometimes she asks me to call ahead for her. "Find out if Rev'rend Peacock is there. I only want to talk to him. No one else." I phone in Ada's reservation. But many times she walks in, looks the place over, turns around, and walks out. "Rev'rend Peacock, he was on the phone." But couldn't she have waited for him? "They got too many men over there. I can't stay there. It make my side hurt so *bad*."

"But you like Jennifer and Joan," I say. "They're not going to let anything bad happen to you."

"My side hurts when I go in there," Ada says. "There's just too many men there."

Ada has applied for Section #8 Housing. Apartments for the poor. They cost exactly one quarter of a person's income. For Ada, that will be $117 a month, one fourth of her SSI check. The apartments are way out in the Bushwick section of Brooklyn. We're in lower Manhattan, at least an hour away.

Ada's been telling me for months that she's on a waiting list for one of these apartments. Of course, she also tells me that she is being followed by people who track her through radio contact with an electrode implanted in her side, so it's hard for me to evaluate the status of her Section #8 application solely on the basis of her report. "They say it gonna be sometime within the next thirty days," she says excitedly, and thirty days come and go. No apartment.

I don't know how to handle Ada's hope. I picture myself five years from now, still sitting here with Ada, listening to her tell me that her apartment will be ready in thirty days. She wants me to be excited with her. But I am afraid to talk about it. I am afraid to meet Ada's eyes when another thirty days have elapsed and she's still on the ferry. And I am full of anger. This woman is ill. She's got no business living on the Staten Island Ferry. What's wrong with us that we can't protect her from her own nightmares and what they do to her? How on earth is Ada ever going to negotiate the red tape of the housing office? Well-balanced college graduates have a hard time making it in New York. How is a paranoid schizophrenic with an eighth-grade education going to live here? I wish she'd never left Alabama.

The end of the month is the hardest. "I hate to ask," Ada says, and I give her some money. She hasn't been able to make her money last. I think of the monochromatic outfits. Maybe if Ada didn't go to thrift shops. But then I think of her on the ferry in the night, lurching awake every fifteen minutes as the boat slams into the dock, and of her gray face the morning after a night like that. And of the time her eye was bloody.

Sometimes Ada checks into a hotel for a few days at the beginning of the month. Forty dollars a night. She carries a brochure about the hotel in her bag. In it there's a picture of her room: A pale blue satin bedspread. Garish pictures on the walls. She shows me the picture proudly. "I stayed there lots of times. They give you two towels every morning. It's real nice." Sometimes she stays there until she runs out of money. She runs out of money before she runs out of month. She carries the picture with her until the beginning of the next month.

On a Monday morning, Ada is waiting for me when I arrive at the office. "I got my paper from housing!" she says, and shoves a wrinkled paper into my hand. I read it. It *is* her housing paper. It says she's approved for Section #8. She has to find a place. They have to inspect it. Then she'll get it. It will be in about thirty days, she says. Right. But it *is* there on the paper. And the paper *is* from the housing office.

A few days later, she's back. She has a business proposition. "I've found me a place," she says. And she really has. Two bedrooms in a complex that rents lots of Section #8 housing. But here's the catch: they want one month's security and one month's rent. Plus an application fee and something called a "key deposit." I can't believe this. One month's security and one month's rent from someone whose total income is $465 a month? And what the hell is a "key deposit?" How come I didn't have to pay a key deposit on *my* apartment? Are any homeless people able to swing this? I don't see how.

Ada asks me for the money. One hundred seventeen times two, plus twenty-five, plus seventy-five. Almost three hundred fifty dollars. "That's a lot of money, Ada," I say. And it is. It's December. I don't have anything left in my discretionary fund. If I do this, it's going to be on me. "I'll pay you back," she says, and I know that she will try to do that. She usually pays me back at least part of what I give her. That's more than most people do.

I call the housing office. And the apartment rental place, to make sure everything is real. It is. I am no longer afraid of Ada's hope. And so I give her the money. "*Don't lose this!*" I say as she tucks it into her bag. "This is the end of being homeless for you." Ada giggles and kisses me. She says something about my being a real mother. Or a real idiot, I say to myself as she goes out the door. I've just given a crazy person $350. For all I know, I've just invested in a dozen red rag outfits. Or a week in a fleabag hotel. I pray that she and the money make it to the apartment complex. Somehow, I think they will.

And they do. On Sunday she is in church. She shows Jack Moody the keys to her apartment. "I got me a place," she beams. There is no furniture in Ada's apartment. She has no food—we find some donated canned goods and she carries them home. Someone gives her a blanket and a sheet. She has found a chair in the garbage. She sits on her chair and looks out the window of her house as the sun sets over Bushwick.

TO BE OR NOT TO BE

ONE OF THE THINGS that everybody "knows" is that the medical profession has an arsenal of sophisticated machinery that it wants to attach to dying people so that their misery can be prolonged. We "know" that doctors and hospitals years ago abandoned human values in favor of their own technologies, and that there are two choices: death with dignity and death with technology. You don't have both.

And so at dinner parties and in the employees' lounge at work, you will often hear robust middle-aged people holding forth emphatically about where they stand on extraordinary life-saving measures. "I don't want to be hooked up to any machines," they announce. "You all heard it here. If I ever get sick, just let me go. I don't want to die all full of tubes."

I have heard people say that they wouldn't want to live if they were paralyzed. And I have heard others say that they wouldn't want to live if they were confined to a wheelchair. I know one man who wouldn't want to live if he couldn't make love to his wife. I even know a young woman who wouldn't want to live if she had to take medicine every day. What these people all have in common is that none of them are in the situations they have judged would make their lives unlivable. They're in terrific shape. But they've read about people maintained in chronic vegetative states, or they visited someone once who was on a respirator. Or they had a relative who suffered through chemotherapy. And they have assumed that the worst case is the only case in the use of these technologies. They have assumed that all comas are irreversible. That all drug side effects are devastating, and the drugs themselves of no avail. That a quadriplegic is functionless. That a person in a wheelchair is helpless. And so they have rushed to a policy statement: anything less than perfect health is a reason for wanting to die.

I've visited people in hospitals for many years. I've seen many people in tragic, hopeless situations. I have seen many people die. I remember a young woman I visited every week for a year. She had gone into respiratory arrest during a caesarean section and never regained consciousness. The baby survived, and there was another child at home, a two-year-old. The woman lay in a fetal position with her mouth open, always the same way. She did not respond to any stimulus. Her mother came every day with a tape recorder, on which she played her daughter's favorite tunes over and over again. Never once was there an indication that she heard them. She breathed, of course, because a machine helped her breathe. She was fed through tubes, medicated through tubes, and her bodily wastes were eliminated through tubes. It was a terrible thing. After a year, she died of pneumonia.

But, as sad as it was, the decision to use these extraordinary means to save her life was one that had to be made. Medical emergencies happen fast. Decisions about handling them have to be made on the spot, and the outcome of a decision like that is never known in advance. And so a healthy young woman with two little children who need their mother stops breathing. The doctors and nurses don't turn to one another and say, "What do you think? Do you think she'd want to be hooked up to tubes?" They get moving and get her breathing, so that if there is brain function left they can save it. Her death is by no means certain because she has had respiratory arrest. Or because she is in a coma. People come out of a coma and return to normal function all the time. And they are able to do it because of these machines. It's like most things. Sometimes it works and sometimes it doesn't.

I've known young people who say they don't want to get old. I rarely meet an old person who doesn't want to get older. A man says that he hopes his father won't last long in his present condition. He's eighty-three, and very frail. I just don't think he's very happy, he says. What he means is that *he* is not happy seeing his dad that way, and doesn't think he would be happy if he himself were in that state. And yes, the father *is* unhappy at his weakness. Wishes it were otherwise. But being unhappy is not the same thing as wanting to die. He wants very much to live. He is willing to do whatever it takes to do so. That's what he wants.

People who have health and strength think that it is those things that make life worth living. And they do make life sweet. But life itself has value, even when the quality of life is radically diminished. Being part of the only world we know anything about matters intensely to us, and people are usually braver than they ever would have expected to be as they struggle to hang on to it. They don't feel they no longer exist because they can't walk, or because of the frustration of being unable to talk. They know they do exist, even if they only know it by virtue of their sorrow at what they have lost, and they are surprised by how much existence matters. And then they surprise themselves again, when they are brave enough to begin to want to say goodbye to life. But they usually do it gradually, as their bodies become less and less able to contain their spirits. There does come a time when a person feels trapped in a body he no longer wants, and he wants to leave. Death is then no longer an enemy, but a friend. But the threshold of that desire for escape is a lot higher than the well usually think it is. And so you sometimes find a person who had come out strongly against the use of machines to save lives when he was healthy changing his mind when he gets sick. He wants to live.

We visit my mother-in-law at Christmas. She has Alzheimer's disease. She rarely knows where she is. She recognizes none of her attendants. My husband is the only person she knows consistently, and sometimes she confuses even him with her doctor. When she realizes that she has done that, she is filled with despair. Often she calls for her mother to come and help her. Her mother has been dead for forty years.

We have brought a home Communion set with us—a tiny chalice and paten, like doll dishes, with little cruets of water and wine and a little box for the wafers, all in a black leather box the size of a recipe file. We set out the dishes on her hospital table, and we begin. My husband reads from the King James version of the Bible, the one we thought she'd be likeliest to remember. "And it came to pass in those days that there went out a decree from Caesar Augustus that all the world should be taxed . . ." She listens intently. For the service itself, we use the 1928 edition of the Book of Common Prayer, which is no longer used much in public worship but was the one she knew years ago. She listens again, and repeats whole prayers—long, involved ones in Elizabethan English—from memory. I stumble once—I've not used the '28 in a long time—and she carries on with the correct words until I find my place. She cannot remember the day of the week or the name of the president or even her last meal, but these ancient words are still there. They are branded in her failing mind. When it is time to receive the bread and wine, she holds up her hands in the shape of a cross as she was taught to do when she was little.

When the service is over, she says, "Thank you very much." I know that she does not know who I am. I thank her for sharing the worship with us, and her son makes a little joke with her about her good memory of all those old words. She smiles and nods slightly. She has already forgotten what we have just done. After a few more minutes, we wheel her back out to the common room, where a group of people in wheelchairs sit in front of the television, and say good-bye.

Her husband is dead, and she lives in a world perpetually new and strange to her. She is often aware of the fact that her memory is gone, and her sorrow and frustration at this are profound. Apart from her failing memory, she is in pretty good health. She may live a long time yet. That is not a happy thought. Hers is not a happy life.

But even she has never said that she wants to die. The duty and desire to live is ingrained in her, and she has not transcended it. As she worsens, she will begin to do that, and nature will begin to take its course toward death. Nobody will be sorry. But, for now, the will of the organism to survive prevails. And she grasps what pleasures remain, pitifully few in number: her memories of beautiful old prayers, her meals, a song on the radio by Fred Astaire. Not much more than that. But she is alive.

A book of recipes for taking one's own life made it to the top of the *New York Times* best-seller list. People were of several minds about it. My life is my own, said some, and it's nobody's business but mine when it ends. Others were nervous about the book, afraid that thousands who were just having bad days would go home, whip up a lethal milkshake in the blender, and end it all. And there will be some of that. People who are suicidally depressed and could be treated will read this book, and they will find a tragically permanent solution to a temporary problem.

But there won't be very many of them. People are born wanting to live, and most of them keep on wanting to live. They want to be well and strong, but they are willing to be sick and weak if they can just go on being part of the life of the world. They surprise themselves and others with how much they want this. Everybody wants to be happy. But almost everyone wants even more simply to be.

IF I SHOULD DIE BEFORE I WAKE

I REMEMBER THE WAITING for the birth of my first child. I remember sitting on my bed with my best friend, holding up baby clothes and laughing about how small they were. And then I remember how lost my baby was in those same tiny clothes the first time I put them on her. She was so much smaller than I thought she would be. Older women said, "Oh, a nice, big baby!" when they learned that she weighed over eight pounds. *Big?* I was glad I didn't get one of the small ones. Those tiny hands, the useless little feet, each with five little toes like five pearls, the paper-thin ears—so tiny. So fragile. I was forever checking the crib to see if she was still breathing, forever calling the doctor or my mother at every whimper, every rash, uncertain and unwilling to trust my instincts. Perhaps I am doing something wrong. Maybe there's something wrong with the baby and I'm too inexperienced to recognize it. Maybe it's just colic and needs to be cried through. But maybe it's something else and needs medical attention. Maybe it's teething pain. Or maybe it's too early for teeth and it's some other kind of pain. How can I tell?

Luckily, the anxiety that comes with first babies doesn't last long. No mother can hold her breath for twenty years, although some of us have had babies whom we thought perhaps could. Time and familiarity enable the instinctive equipment parents have for taking care of their children to work automatically, and we relax. We learn which cry means something's wrong and which is just making conversation. We learn to do the things we know are best and to wait confidently for the results. We learn to trust ourselves more, and to relax.

But we never relax completely. The anxiety that a brand-new mother or father faces comes from an unrealistic expectation that the parent can control every second of the child's life and is therefore responsible for making every second an experience in pure joy. That goes away, and we learn to allow our children to grow with a little less monitoring. But we pay a price for this relaxation. Relinquishing our imagined total control over our children's every moment means that we admit that there are *other* forces in their lives, forces not at our disposal. Forces we do not control. Separateness without love is easy. Separateness *with* love, though, recognizing that my child is a separate person with a destiny separate from my own, a destiny I cannot completely control: that's frightening. That's the kind of anxiety that comes into play when it's three o'clock in the morning and your teenager was going to be home at eleven. When your child is failing in school and the teacher says the ability is there but he's just not trying. When your child has persistent headaches and the doctor says he wants to run some tests. The mothers of toddlers sit on the park bench and watch a sullen teenager go by. "My child will never be like that," they think, and congratulate themselves in advance on the perfect job of parenting they will do. But already there is a warning inside. Can I be so sure? A mature recognition of the separateness of parents and children is a scary thing. The knowledge that there will be things in their world that you cannot control carries with it a well-founded fear. You used to lie awake worrying about whether you had introduced rice cereal a week too soon. Now you know other fears at night. The stakes are a lot higher. Fears that don't spring from a neurotic need to control everything, but from an accurate assessment of what the world is like. The world is sometimes a dangerous place in which to live. There are things out there that can really hurt your child. And so, you worry.

When you worry, you experience every bad thing twice: once while you're worrying about the possibility of its happening, and then again when it does. If it's true—and it *is* true—that most of the situations our children will face are going to be situations over which our control is severely limited, what kind of peace of mind can we have without lying to ourselves?

First, the bad news. For our children—and for ourselves—the journey of life is still a journey into death, and the road upon which that journey is taken is a rough road. And, often, a terribly unfair one. I remember a woman who threw out all the crucifixes from her Catholic home when her son was killed in Vietnam. She had thought she had an agreement with God that her son would be saved, and her anger was savage when that agreement was broken. It's not that way. To think that entrusting our children to God or anything else is an end run around trouble invites despair. For our kids, and for us, there is going to be suffering. If some suffering is inevitable—and it is—then what one *does* with suffering becomes all-important. Suffering that is mute, that cannot reflect upon itself and be conscious of itself and be grown through: such suffering is in vain. Peace of mind is not the absence of suffering. Peace of mind is growth and deepening in the face of—and sometimes, though we may fight against the thought, even *because* of—suffering. Who are our kids going to call upon when they fall? Us? To whom will their anger be directed when life is hard? Us? We who are as helpless as they in the face of it all? No way.

Now I lay me down to sleep,
I pray the Lord my soul to keep.
If I should die before I wake
I pray the Lord my soul to take.

There are probably prayers more helpful to children at bedtime than this one, which reinforces the childhood suspicion that going to sleep is somehow like dying. But theologically it's pretty on-target: sleeping or waking, life *is* uncertain and sometimes it is also painful. They'd better know this, and know that we know it, too, that pain is a part of life, and an exception will not be made in their case. Worry will dominate them, as it did us when they were tiny, unless we show them how to live with the uncertainty of life.

So what will we do? Tell them to trust God and then fold our hands and wait for the end, like the parents you read about every once in a while who don't believe in doctors and stand by in prayer while their children die from some preventable disease? No. We love them too much, and we respect whatever wisdom and skill we *do* possess too much. We're not God, but we *are* moms and dads. We give them everything we have. Our lives, if it should come to that, without even thinking twice about it. Oh, yes. In a minute.

But then, after we've done all we could, we've got to turn it over. You can't do more than your best. You can't give more than you've got. The rest is not up to you. And, whatever that means to you, when you can go no further, that's where you are.

Poor lady, with her crucifixes out in the trash can, full of fury and love for her dead son. Raging at the one who, we are told, watched *his* son die for three hours, pinned to a wooden cross like a captured butterfly. I remember that she said to me, "It's *sick*. To have those things in the house—it's just *sick*." All those strong young men on crosses, young men with everything to live for, nailed on crosses—she refused to glory in the cross, as her upbringing had taught her to do. She may not have had her son anymore, but at least she had her anger. And her love. And she knew the difference between right and wrong. And she knew that losing him was wrong. As loss is always wrong. No glory in it. Just wrong.

Am I saying that there is ultimately no way to protect these children whom we love more than we love our own lives from death? Yes, I guess that's what I am saying. Am I saying that God isn't going to do that either? Yes, I guess I'm saying that, too. In the end, we all die. And some of us die too soon. I guess I am saying that. Life happens. Death happens. Our anxiety won't influence what happens much one way or the other. But accepting what happens—not permitting it, for our permission is not asked, but accepting it—is the only way we can take any joy at all in what we have.

When I was a child, a volcano erupted unexpectedly in Iceland, burying a small town at the foot of its cone. All of the children in the town were in school at the time, and they all perished. The parents sent their sons and daughters out the door that morning, same as they always did, and never saw them again.

I remember my mother being profoundly moved by that tragedy. She always made sure that the last words we had in the morning were loving ones. That cannot always have been easy, but my memory is that she usually succeeded. When I had children myself, she told me about this rule of hers, and about those children in Iceland. I remembered it dimly. She couldn't shake it. She said that I should always remember that today could be the last day. Tell your children you love them every day. Just in case. It might be the last chance you have to tell them, she said. You don't know.

I didn't experience this as morbid. I didn't then, and I don't now. I think it's realistic. You don't know. So you'd better love what you have while you have it. Nothing can ever take the moment you have before you away. It will always *have been.* Take it. It's yours. It is the only one you will ever have.

THE SAINT OF LOST THINGS

TO COME UPON THE BASILICA of Saint Anthony at night is like finding oneself in a child's dream of the Middle Ages. It looks like nothing else in Italy. It has minarets and Moorish-looking domes, seven or eight of them, although it gives the impression that there are dozens, as if the church were not a church at all but a fairy-tale city of immense size. The night sky above Padua is deep indigo blue, undimmed by competing light from the ground, and the basilica stands red against it, red as a ruby, much redder than it really is. A *lot* of things about the basilica seem more magnificent than they really are. It is certainly an unusually beautiful piece of medieval architecture—but there is no shortage of that in Italy. It is certainly large—but there are many larger. It is sumptuously appointed—but many Italian churches are more so. It isn't even the art history champion of its own city—that honor surely belongs to the Scrovegni chapel, with its famous Giotto frescoes of the life of Christ. Yet there is something miraculous about Saint Anthony's church, something undefinable. Oh, yes, says everyone I've ever talked to who has visited Padua, I know what you mean.

I suppose it has to do with the saint himself, and the busloads of people arriving every day to petition him. The patron of the lost things. He sleeps inside the basilica, his enormous stone sarcophagus drawing the visitor to the east end from the moment of entering the church. And all around him walk the faithful, as close to the saint as they can get, close enough to touch the stone, to kiss it if they can. They often leave a message of thanks or a prayer behind. And photographs. Pictures of shaken young men standing, unscathed, beside their totaled cars. Walked away from the accident without a scratch. A miracle. A visit to the shrine of Saint Anthony to leave documentation behind. Hundreds of such photographs, from all over the world, of smiling people holding unneeded crutches aloft, of children who were not expected to live, blowing out birthday candles or making their first Communions. A pink knitted bonnet and sweater, worn by a baby whose parents had given up all hopes of ever having a child, brought to Padua from Trieste and left there in thanksgiving.

And hundreds of letters requesting the saint's help in new lost causes—one from a couple in Pennsylvania who have tried every medical treatment known for their daughter's leukemia. Another from a woman in Canada, paralyzed from the waist down. She has consulted many doctors, and they all concur: she will not walk again. It is official: there is now nowhere else to turn. Perhaps Saint Anthony can help.

My husband and I sit drinking coffee in a café across the piazza from where the basilica glows against the sky. He took the afternoon to nose about in the museum next to Saint Anthony's. I took the afternoon off. He is full of a combination of bemusement and energy that is uniquely his, and which is the thing I love most about him. The museum is full of the things people have left here, he tells me. A history of the cult of Saint Anthony. Centuries of it. He tells me about a picture, sort of a before-and-after commercial for Saint Anthony. In the first frame, a husband and wife lie stiffly in bed, the covers pulled up to their chins. Their faces are sad. In the second frame, Saint Anthony himself has broken right through the wall, flying into the room in his brown monk's robe, a baby in his arms for the longing parents, who are now all smiles. And another before-and-after, this one of a young girl who fell out of a window. Her mother and other people crowd around her crumpled form, lying on the ground. They are grieving; we know this because their mouths are all identical round *O*'s. And in the next frame the girl stands up, well and strong, her great full skirt ballooning neatly around her without so much as a tear in it, while Saint Anthony stands modestly off to one side, holding his symbols, a book and a lily, the mother kneeling to embrace his feet.

He goes on to describe other artifacts in the museum —long locks of hair shorn from women stricken with fever and offered to the saint when they recovered, crumpled fenders from wrecked cars whose occupants miraculously survived, pieces of wood from shipwrecks—and then for a while we do not speak. We are both thinking of the centuries of hope and longing that have journeyed to the building across the square. No wonder the basilica glows. People in need of healing, willing to go anywhere, do anything, to turn things around. Asking the patron of lost things—lost hope, lost health, lost love—to fly through the solid brick wall of reality and give them their hearts' desires.

He loves to think of that hope, he says after a while. He remembers when he had it. I think of what he lost: a son who died at twenty-seven, quadriplegic after an automobile accident. And of the people I have met since then who also know about lost things. Some of them find the idea of hope offensive, a cruel joke. And yet they have dreams full of it, magical dreams: the dead restored to them, returned to life. "But I thought you were dead!" they say in the dream, unable to believe the miracle. "Oh, no, it was all a mistake," says the dead one gently, and they awaken soaked with a happiness beyond words. But it was only a dream. And they are as bitter as before.

He has those dreams, too. But he does not awaken into

bitterness. To him, they are a gracious break from a sorrow that never leaves him, and he welcomes them. They are worth the fresh pain of waking afterward. This was what it was to hope innocently, before there was such a thing in his life as a lost cause. This was what it was to be touched by a miracle. It doesn't change what is. But it is good to have that feeling for a little while.

I think of a conversation I once had with a woman about her father's death, which had occurred years before. She was still outraged because of the way he had suffered, angry about it. Angry at her sister, whom she felt hadn't visited enough. Angry at her father-in-law because he was still alive. Angry at me because I worked for God, who had let this happen. She was a wealthy woman, beautifully dressed. She wore expensive gold jewelry, and lived in a beautiful house. It was clear that she was accustomed to having the things she wanted, and could not put aside the fury of having been denied something she longed for as much as her father's healing.

Her concern, of course, was with herself. She was innocent, and the world a friendly place, until she herself sustained a loss. Of course, she had known other people who had died. She lived in a century that had seen twelve million people suffer and die in concentration camps. Those deaths had not embittered her. She had still been able to think that a world in which babies had been incinerated alive was a hopeful place. If she had bothered to think about it at all. But when her own father died, she felt a trust had been violated. This isn't supposed to happen to *him*, she cried out to no one. This isn't supposed to happen to *me*. And the fact that it *did* happen is, to this day, an impossible thing for her to forgive. And so now the world, which had seemed so much her friend, is enemy territory.

Philosophers and theologians talk about the problem of evil. Why do bad things happen? Why do they happen to one person and not to another? People who are not philosophers or theologians also talk about the problem of evil. They usually wait to talk about it until they are laid low by something terrible that has occurred in their own lives. They had not thought something like this could happen. Not to them. But then they see it can. Well, of course, most of them eventually come to say, why *not* me? Did I think I was special? I suppose I did think that. But now I see that these things just happen. At random. To anybody.

If there is a problem of evil, then there is also a problem of good. I may not understand why my child died the way he did, but I also don't understand why I was lucky enough to have him in the first place. Both are mysteries. I earned neither. Was entitled to neither. And both happened. Sometimes a wall collapses and kills people. And sometimes Saint Anthony crashes through a wall and brings you a baby. There is no reason to expect one of these things to happen instead of the other. And because they are equally unlikely, there is no reason not to hope. It is a happier choice than despair, and it is no less grounded in reality. So people go on doing it.

A busload of pilgrims pulls up in front of the basilica. The people begin to pile out: Husbands and wives in rumpled travel clothes. A large group of sisters, some in white habits, others in pale blue skirts and white blouses. Priests in black. Several of the people hold white envelopes. Pictures and letters about their hopes, which they will leave with the saint of lost things. They stand and gaze in wonder at Saint Anthony's, at the towers that seem to go on forever, like the city of God. And then they go inside.

♦

THE THINGS KIDS SAY

♦

WHEN I WAS LITTLE, I thought Boston was a state, not a city. I thought that for a long time, until I was about eight, and my brother confronted me with the truth. There it was in black and white in a geography book: Boston was not a state, after all; it was a city in Massachusetts. I was furious. It sounded like a state. I had been sure it was a state. And now here I was, mistaken, and my brother was right.

When my mother was little, she thought the Roman emperors had been called "Kaisers," not "Caesars." She had heard a great deal about the Kaiser when she was tiny, and she thought that was how "Caesar" was pronounced for a long time, until she was embarrassed by her mistake while reading aloud one day at school. Her sister Harriet thought that veal came from little animals with two hooved feet, long fur, and heads like pigs. She thought that because her father had told her so, with his deadpan Scandinavian delivery. Aunt Harriet thought there was such a thing as a veal until she was twelve or thirteen.

My daughter thought that smoke detectors *caused* fires when she was little. She went through a period of hiding the smoke detector every day. She'd take it down and put it in a drawer in her room, or in her closet. Took her life in her own hands, as far as she was concerned, to save her family. For all she knew, it was ready to burst into flames at any moment. She couldn't understand why we chose to have such a dangerous thing in the house. Her dad remembers thinking, when he was little, that firemen went around town starting fires. He was constantly on the lookout for them on his street, ready to give the alarm if he saw one.

Children apply the best thinking they can come up with to the things they see around them. They take immense time and trouble to figure things out, often without all the facts and without knowing all the rules. And so they sometimes get funny results. But they're in there thinking and puzzling the best they can.

What trips them up is lack of information and an inability to reason logically. These are things that come with age. They come at fairly definite stages, and they're just not there before they come. The things that kids think make us laugh precisely because we can see how they got there: it isn't correct to think that firemen start fires, but we can see why a kid might think it was. The emperors of Rome were not called "Kaisers," but we can see why a little girl who was three when the First World War began thought they were. Kids make sense in their own way.

Everybody has heard of the little boy who pledged allegiance to the republic "where the witches stand." What a picture *that* must have conjured up in his mind. And the little girl who prayed, "Our Father, who art in heaven, Howard be thy name." It didn't seem out of the question for God to have a name. One wonders how she responded to the first person she met whose name was Howard, though. Eventually somebody picks up the mistake and the child corrects it. But she never forgets that once upon a time, familiar words meant something different.

So many things go into the images we carry in our minds. Things we saw and heard when we were young. Before we could talk, even. I look at my grandchildren and wonder where they will come out as they try to think things through. The little one chatters away in long paragraphs, inflecting them in very precise ways. They are not in any language I know, but she is clearly talking. She assumes that if she makes animated noises and thinks the things she wants to say, people will understand her. The older one has an impressive command of the English language, and is very thoughtful about words. There are a few things of which she is unsure. She learns that a friend has moved to a place called Frenchtown. Does she speak French now, Rosie wants to know. That's a fair question. They both will carry different images out of their childhoods from the ones I carried out of mine. I doubt that there is anything I could do that would give them the simple picture of a mother and her baby that I associated with the word "Madonna" when I was a child. That's over.

We all carry the images of what we saw when we were children. We also carry with us some other things from back then, things that are not so funny and endearing. Some of us learned as small children to be afraid of the world, taught to be so by someone older than we were who was also afraid. Some of us learned to devalue ourselves when we were young, learned not to see our own beauty, learned to apologize too often, to apologize for things that were not our fault. Some of us learned that we never quite measured up, that what was required of us was a perfection we knew we could never in a million years attain. I know beautiful people who think they are homely. Intelligent people who think they are stupid. Productive people who think they are lazy. They've carried these false valuations of themselves from childhood. They don't pledge allegiance to the republic where the witches stand anymore, but they still lug these things around.

Mistakes may be charming or they may be tragic, but they are always mistakes. They get in the way. They make us less than we can be. They've all got to go. Nobody's going to let a child go on thinking that smoke detectors start fires. Or that God is a guy named Howard. They've got to know the truth. And they've got to know the truth about those other things, too, so that their lives are more full of joy than of guilt or shame.

THE QUIET HOUR CLUB

THE QUIET HOUR CLUB was founded in 1895. Its purpose was "to bring together the women in Metuchen, N. J. for mental culture, social intercourse, and a sympathetic understanding of whatever women are doing along the best lines of progress." There were eight charter members. Then, as now, membership in Quiet Hour was by nomination. One did not apply.

Meetings were held on alternate Thursday afternoons. They still are. According to the bylaws of the club, members must attend all meetings or be explicitly excused. A member must host a meeting every two years, and must present an original paper every year. Associate members—those who have become too frail to fulfill these obligations, or those who have moved away—are permanently excused.

I am told that there was a time when the rules were fiercely upheld. Latecomers were greeted with a chilly blanket of disapproval. A certain number of unexcused absences was ground for expulsion from Quiet Hour. Women had to raise their hands and be recognized before they could speak. Fortunately, things have loosened up considerably. Otherwise, I'd have been out on my ear years ago. The insanity of my work schedule makes it impossible for me to attend more than two meetings a year: the one at which I speak and, when it is my turn, the one I host. I try to remember to write in the fall and ask for a standing excuse. Sometimes, I forget to do even that, and on an occasional Thursday afternoon I look up from my work and imagine the silence after my name is called in the roll, and I wish I were there. I am always politely dunned for my tardy membership dues, and I am always embarrassed. When I am the hostess, the fare is more likely to have emerged from a white cardboard baker's box than from my oven. I know that I am the Maria von Trapp of the organization. But the women of the club seem to take my shortcomings as a member with good grace. On those rare occasions when I am there, I feel welcome.

And I am glad to be there. More glad than the experience warrants, as a matter of fact. It's just a women's club in a suburban town. But it's delicious to me: an afternoon tea, a rare chance to use my silver. Women in suits and silk blouses. The buzz of their chatter, the inevitable jokes about the noisiness of Quiet Hour. The careful running of the meeting, its gentle but firm use of parliamentary procedure. The familiar litany of the roll call: no first names here. "Mrs. Stapley?" "Present." "Mrs. Stone?" "Present." It is predictable. It is dutiful. It hasn't changed all that much in its century of common life. Everyone who has ever been a member is listed in its program. I am listed there, too.

Today, the second Thursday in December, I am the hostess of the holiday meeting. I did not tell the people at work what I was taking the day off for. They probably think I am resting and writing. But I am polishing silver, my mother's coffee service, and my mother-in-law's sugar bowls, oddly shaped and unmatched. The little silver filigree candy dish shaped like a heart, which I thought was the most beautiful object in the world when I was seven. The silver teapot that sits on a stand so that you don't have to lift it when you pour. It has a little silver candle holder in the bottom so the tea stays warm. It used to belong to a Quiet Hour member, an unmarried lady who, when she entered a nursing home, gave it to another member who, when *she* moved to a retirement home in Texas, gave it to me. It's one of the most elegant things I've ever owned. I survey the table I have set, wish I hadn't taken my mother's china cup collection up to New York where it doesn't go with anything, and run to answer the doorbell.

It is Mary. She has come early because she guesses I might need a hand. Mary also sometimes calls me to remind me when I am scheduled to host or to give a paper. Or, if I have lost my Quiet Hour schedule and suspect I may soon be hosting a meeting, I call her. I know she won't think ill of me for being a mess. More than once, she has saved me from forgetting to include a Quiet Hour meeting in my calendar and covering myself with shame. How good she looks, I think, and I tell her so. Her children are all grown up and have children of their own. She has lived in Metuchen for forty years, and has been a member of Quiet Hour for twenty-five of them.

It is now just shy of one o'clock, and members begin to come up the walk by twos and threes. I greet them at the door. We tell each other how long it's been since we've seen each other, and they ask about how things are in New York. "Oh, you know," I say, "noisy and dirty and nothing works." I think of the hurried life I live in Manhattan as I hang up their coats. The meetings, the phone calls, the things that have to be dealt with *rightnow,* the sidewalk cruelties we who live there must helplessly behold every day. Another world.

I commute back and forth between the kitchen and the living room, which is now filled with women. Every chair we own is in there, and every chair is taken. The meeting has begun. There are minutes from the last meeting, and a treasurer's report. These are always pretty quiet—not much action in the treasury. The club's major expense is the occasional purchase of a book for the public library in memory of a Quiet Hour member who has died. Today there are two such memorials in the report. A member reads a short statement about the deceased: where she was educated, how long she had been a Quiet Hour member, what her interests and enthusiasms were ("she was a gourmet cook, and on many occasions the members of the Quiet Hour Club enjoyed her creations after meetings at her gracious home"). Each memorial closes with an expression of sorrow at the club's loss of a devoted member and sympathy to the husbands and children who survive. Someone moves the entering of these reports into the Quiet Hour minutes. We remember the faces of those women whose memorial volumes will soon be in the town library. Someday each of us will have a book there with her name in it. Someday, I guess, I will have one.

Now the first paper is being read. It is Mary's. It is called "The Glory of a Garden," and it's about ancient Babylon. I can hear her voice from the kitchen, where I am fussing with the coffee. It is light and young, for a grandmother of eleven. Mary dreads giving her paper every year, or says she does. Many of the members say the same thing. They work hard on these projects, choosing them a year in advance from a general topic upon which the club has agreed to draw. This year the topic is "Wonders of the World." I am doing Chartres Cathedral. But I have until April. I think.

Because this is the holiday meeting, we sing Christmas carols after both papers have been applauded. My piano is in New York now, so we are a capella. The women's voices harmonize sweetly as the winter sunlight begins to gray and the room begins to darken a little. It is cold outside. But the smell of coffee fills the house wonderfully, and as we sing the old songs again, we are warm. The eight charter members sang these songs at their Christmas meeting in 1895. Some club members' mothers sang them at Christmas meetings in the twenties. Busy with families and preparations for Christmas day, the women of the Quiet Hour Club savor the pause in their activity this Thursday afternoon, the last meeting before Christmas in the club's ninety-fifth year.

OUR LADY

WHEN THE BLESSED MOTHER GAVE birth to her baby in the stable at Bethlehem, she wore a simple linen shirt. Mary must have been the kind who never threw anything away; she seems to have kept the shirt throughout her life. Naturally, after she died, it didn't seem *right* just to throw away a shirt that had belonged to the Blessed Mother, even if she didn't need it anymore. So the shirt was preserved. For several centuries, it made the rounds of the faithful along with lots of other relics —saints' toes, shoulder sockets, fingers—until it ended up in the cathedral of Chartres. It is still there, its sleeves folded neatly over the arms of a stand in a glass box. It is called the *sancta camisia*—the holy shirt.

The presence of the shirt made a big difference in life at Chartres. Since its donation by Charles the Bald in 876, it was the most precious of Chartres's many precious possessions. It symbolized Mary's actual presence in the cathedral. As the Middle Ages continued, the cathedral at Chartres became more and more important as a pilgrim shrine. It was not only one of the many churches dedicated to Mary. It was *the* Mary church, her home. In 1194, when a fire burned and heavily damaged the cathedral, and the citizens of Chartres were in despair at this clear sign that the Blessed Mother had abandoned them, just at the time when their spirits were at their lowest, lo, up from the crypt came a procession of priests and acolytes and torchbearers and thurifers and other holy personnel—and the bishop, who carried the shirt. Good as new, and completely unharmed by the fire. Now there was a sign a person could get enthusiastic about. And they did.

They set about rebuilding the cathedral. And they set about it with such energy and singleness of purpose that it was completed in just thirty years' time. For the sole purpose of comparison and not to be critical at all, let me point out that the National Cathedral in Washington, D.C., took one hundred years to build, and the Cathedral Church of Saint John the Divine in New York City, which was begun in 1895, is far from finished *yet*. And the builders of *those* mammoth churches had paved streets and locomotives and heavylift cranes.

The people of Chartres yoked themselves to huge sledges, in groups of a thousand at a time, to drag the blocks of granite from the quarry five miles away. If we are to believe contemporary sources, nobleman and peasant strained against the load side by side, pulling the heavy stone along what roads there were in that part of twelfth-century France. The kings of England contributed richly to the rebuilding of Chartres, even though they were at war with the kings of France much of the time. Of all the churches outside England endowed by the English throne, Chartres received the most generous gifts. Everyone who was anyone in Europe was solicited for money, and everyone came across.

People dropping what they were doing and hitching themselves to wagons, like beasts of burden. Laborers who worked like slaves all week long, working just as hard on what little time they called their own to finish the church. Monarchs setting aside considerations of war and peace to adorn Mary's church. Rich and poor alike obsessed with this great project. There is nothing in our age to compare with this sustained and passionate human enterprise. The occasional war may fuse us together, but never for more than a few years. Not for thirty years of building a church by hand.

The other thing that was going on at the same time Chartres was being rebuilt, of course, was a series of Crusades, in which kings and soldiers from European countries made it their business to go east and kill The Turk. They were enthusiastically urged on by the popes, for reasons that must have been clear to everyone at the time but that seem very murky—and not terribly theological—to us.

Each major rebuilding campaign at Chartres, in fact, coincided with one of these Crusades, give or take a few years. You can see the soldiers in the windows at Chartres, as you can in many other places in France. And on the battlefield, you would have seen the Virgin, too, or at least you would have heard her name as a battle cry. Mary was a queen to those who told themselves they were fighting for her, like the queen of France. Never mind that ancient shirt, whose threadbare cloth is so rustic. Mary was a queen, dispensing victory in battle and comfort in the afterlife, approachable by the people in a way that her Son apart from her was not. At Chartres, the Trinity is of little interest, a puzzle for theologians to worry with, not us. Even Christ is considered as much in relation to his mother as on his own at Chartres. An important series of carvings depicting the life of Christ on the Royal Portal—the front door of the entire church—leaves out the Crucifixion. The carvers' attention was focused elsewhere: on their own interesting society—their teachers and craftsmen, their bakers and shoemakers and carpenters and fishmongers, their kings and queens, their famous scholars, poets, and musicians, all carved in the stone and pictured in the glass of Chartres—and on their conviction that the Mother of God was with all those people and would prosper them. We know this when we see what they did at Chartres. How rich it was. How much money it cost. And how quickly—feverishly, really—they worked to create this house for the Virgin.

Whatever the theologians were doing, whatever the soldiers were doing in the Holy Land, Mary lived at Chartres. And still does. The solicitude with which her cousin Elizabeth leans toward her in a carving on the North Porch (we know it's Elizabeth because she looks like Mary, only with crow's-feet and wrinkled cheeks to show her age), the anxiety in Mary's outstretched arms as she looks on while her baby is circumcised in a carving three centuries later: these snapshots come from different worlds, but the femininity of their point of view is the same. Homely scenes adorn the sixteenth-century screen around the choir: Of Mary as a shy child being coaxed up the stairs of the temple by her father. Mary showing the new baby to a trio of chubby toddler angels, patiently listening to one of them who is obviously asking a question. Mary's friends, well-dressed young women of the French Renaissance like Mary herself, coming to spend the afternoon and help with the baby's bath. In the Mary cult, whether it was Mary the queen or Mary the homemaker, people saw their own world. And they believed that she lived in it, and could intervene in it.

The French believed this longer than other people did. While Shakespeare was writing *Henry IV* for his thoroughly secular English audience and to flatter the Virgin Queen, the king and queen of France were traveling fifty miles on foot to Chartres, to petition the Virgin Mother for a child. They didn't get one. We know about that, too: modern people know all about unanswered prayers. At Chartres, and much more as one travels closer to Paris, one notices that somebody has chopped the heads off of a lot of these old statues. Faith turned to rage when poor people began to think that there should be more in life than the promise of something nice later on, and began to sense that the church and the monarchy had used their hope against them.

It was the blacksmiths and the tanners and the bakers and the cobblers who fill the windows of Chartres who rose up in revolution against the rich. The church and its mythology? Mary and her holy shirt and her court and her protection? They hadn't worked. Those were the last things the people wanted. The cathedral at Chartres became, for a spell, a "Temple of Reason." A famous wooden statue of Mary—Our Lady of the Crypt—was burned in front of the Royal Portal. There was talk of tearing the church down altogether. Fortunately, the Reign of Terror ended before that could happen.

It is this remembered bitterness that has led us, the grandchildren of those angry people, to expect that revolutionary fervor will always be antispiritual. But it's not. In Latin America it's Catholic as all get-out, and Mary, she who has always been the one to whom the lowly turned, is involved. People remember that it was she who sang a song about the hungry being filled with good things and the rich being sent away empty. About the humble and meek being exalted and the mighty being tumbled from their thrones. That she was an unwed mother in a patriarchal culture long before anybody ever thought she was a queen. That she was a mother whose son was murdered for political reasons, like the Latin American mothers whose children have been "disappeared." Perhaps she is not a queen after all. Perhaps she is just a friend of the poor. Even at Chartres, the statue of her as queen of heaven was burned. For some reason the simple old shirt, worn by a young girl from a poor family, was not. Maybe there is room for revolution in the stone and the stained glass in this beautiful place, where the sun sends colored light from the height of the windows to the stone floor, where the Blessed Mother looks eternally at her son across the transept, and the people in the stone carvings, most of them at eye level, or at least low enough that we can see them well, look like us.

THE SECOND TIME AROUND

MY FATHER MARRIED my stepmother on his seventy-sixth birthday. She was seventy-five. They stood in the sanctuary of her church and repeated the beautiful old words: ". . . for better for worse, for richer for poorer, in sickness and in health, till death do us part." She wore a cornflower-blue dress, which she had made herself and which matched her eyes. He was soldierly and erect, handsome in his dark suit and the new red tie she had bought him, and he held her hand in his and slid a plain gold ring onto her finger.

Fifty years before, he had been the principal of the high school in a little town in North Dakota. She had been the nurse. A picture of him, taken in 1936, shows a husky young man with wavy brown hair and a grave smile, leaning against a car. I haven't seen a picture of her as she was then, but he says she hasn't changed all that much. Her strawberry-blond hair is still bright, her eyes still the same blue, her mouth still humorous, her eyebrows still quizzical. They had been an item in that little town then, the nurse and her serious young man. They had gone for long drives on the prairie. He had walked her home from the movies, strolling slowly down the dark street in the summer. They had talked of marriage. But somehow that wasn't the time, and then other things got in the way. The war. A continent's-width separation. He married. She married. And for fifty years they had no contact at all.

My mother was named Lorain. She had a dimple in her cheek, which showed irresistibly just before her smile broke across her face. She was bright and optimistic. She played the piano while he sang. He brought her coffee in bed. They ran a house, three children, two grandmothers, and a business together. But as her heart weakened in middle age, her quick step slowed. Her breath failed her. Her hospital stays became discouragingly frequent until at last, almost apologetically, she died. For five years after her death he went through the motions of life, eating and sleeping, working in the garden, picking up the mail, feeling all the while as if he were half alive. He pored over pictures of her, studying her hair, her mouth, willing the feeling of Lorain alive to arise from the picture and enfold him as it once had. But the flatness of the photographs mocked his loneliness, and he felt like a photograph himself. He moved through his days like a visitor to this planet, a detached observer of other peoples' joys and sorrows, a man whose life was over and who was only waiting to die.

Her husband had been named Howard. She had watched as diabetes stole his eyesight bit by bit and then claimed the use of his legs. Howard was funny, even then, and wise. They would sit together in the sunroom of their house, after he could no longer see, and she would read his legal briefs to him so that he could continue his practice. They would drive in the car, she at the wheel, and she would laugh at his criticisms of her driving errors, which, he said, he could *feel*. She had loved putting those vows into practice: "for better, for worse." It had been a privilege to be the one whose support made his productive life possible against such enormous odds. And then, suddenly, there was nothing. She was alone with only the memory of Howard, and she felt lost. With characteristic good sense, she busied herself with her family and her friends and her church. With characteristic firmness and faith, she told herself that Howard was in a place where pain and grief were no more, better off than she ever could have made him. But that was somewhere else, somewhere she could not follow, and her heart ached quietly within her.

There was a reunion of Elgin High School's Class of 1935. Fifty years. The former principal and the former nurse met again in the little drugstore. "Laura?" "Is that you, David?" A brief, flustered exchange. They went for coffee. Disoriented by the unaccustomed feeling of being alive again, he forgot to ask where she was staying. But Elgin is a small town; he found her. They drove again on the prairie. He kissed her again after all those years. He asked her to marry him, and she said yes. And the man who for five years could scarcely be prevailed upon to leave his home flew three thousand miles to a town he'd never seen to marry the woman he'd found again after half a century.

Now the wedding was over, they walked down the aisle, and I watched my father meet his new neighbors, accepting their congratulations with the first joy I'd seen in him in ages. I thought of my mother, that sweet, funny lady, dead these five years. I thought of the pain of his loneliness without her, of the emptiness she had left, of how he had been just putting in time, waiting to die. Of how little use I or anyone else had been in easing that anguish. And now it was gone, finally healed: here he was, full of peace and happiness.

How do the loves of our lives rank, I wondered? Or can we rank them at all? Love between a man and a woman is so exclusive and so unique that the idea that it might be repeated seems, irrationally, to call it into question. I have known adult children who bitterly resented the remarriage of a widowed parent, who saw it as a terrible disloyalty. They seem to have assigned to the surviving parent the job of mourning on behalf of the entire family, and to judge the quality of love during life by the extent to which consolation after death is impossible.

What did our parents do before we came along, we with our banging doors and report cards and braces, with our demands for guidance, freedom, attention, forgiveness?

It is hard for most of us to imagine our parents as people separate from us, they are so important to us as symbols of our nurture and our security. We look at their photographs when they were young, before we came along, before they were married even, and their young faces look back at us with an inexperience we cannot recognize as belonging to our mothers and fathers. Our parents' marriages seem as eternal as rocks to us, the immovable anchors that prove to us that we have a place to which we can always return no matter how far we roam, no matter what we do. *Our* marriages may end, and we may be most insistent on our parents' understanding and support when they do, but we are not always willing to extend the same understanding back. A divorced woman of fifty, for years a successful real estate broker with a home of her own, was furious at her father for having a lady friend a few months after the death of her mother. She railed at the "indecency" of it, refusing to meet the lady or speak to her father, refusing even to speak to a sister who had entertained them in her home. She was living her life of independence and freedom as she had for years, but she depended on her father to burn *his* life as a candle at the shrine of her mother's memory, perhaps so she wouldn't have to burn her own life there. When he stopped cooperating in this one-sided arrangement, stopped doing her grieving for her, she reacted with rage.

There is, in anyone who mourns, an odd pride in the fact of mourning, an impulse to cultivate grief as a fitting tribute to the beloved dead, like the ancient Egyptian practice of shaving one's eyebrows to show bereavement. But a person cannot do that for long without ceasing to be himself, without climbing into a casket of his or her own making, in a useless pantomime of the death of another. Who, observing this in a widowed parent, would not rejoice at its end?

In the church hall after my father's wedding, we ate cake and drank coffee and laughed about my stepmother's sudden acquisition of five grandchildren. And when it was time to leave my father in his new home, I cried as I usually do when I leave him. For our lives. For my mother. For the bittersweet passing of time. But not, for the first time in years, for him.

CLOSING DOWN HOME

I HAVE RENTED a medium-size truck and taken the day off from work. My friend Greg took the day off, too, and we're both wearing the oldest clothes we own. It's not even seven o'clock in the morning when we set off down the New Jersey Turnpike for Maryland, where Greg is going to help me move things out of my childhood home.

It's a three-hour drive—maybe a little longer today, I think, as there is a slight drizzle. I used to drive it all the time when the kids were small. We used to go home for

Thanksgiving and Christmas. As we get closer to my hometown, I feel the same way I have always felt going back. The air feels better down here. The wet leaves on the ground smell different here from the way they smell in New Jersey. The dirt is a different color. The hills and trees we pass are beautiful.

We are very close now. Past the Quaker cemetery, past the pond where I used to go and fish, past the lane that led to my best friend's farm. Past the Grange Hall. I see that it is now a furniture store. Past the gas station and the school. Past the Methodist Church. And into the driveway of our house.

From the outside, it looks the same. The curtains of which my mother was so proud hang in the long windows. The holly I gave my dad for his birthday years ago is gorgeous now—tall and bushy. The lights are on inside, and in the dark November drizzle it looks warm and inviting. If my mother were alive, she'd have heard us turning in the driveway and she'd be on her way to the door now to greet her grandchildren.

But she isn't. She died five years ago. And the kids are in school. It's just Greg and me. I don't believe she ever met Greg. No, of course she didn't; she never knew that we moved to Metuchen, where Greg is our neighbor. Didn't live to see me ordained. Or divorced. Or to see her great-grandchildren. She didn't live to see a lot of things.

But my dad is here. He opens the door and we come in. The place is a mess, but it's clearly in the hands of people who know what they're doing. My stepmother is here, too, her sleeves rolled up for action. They just got married, and they're selling this house. They're going to live in her house in California. So now is the time for us to take the things we want. My father doesn't want much of anything. Some books and a few small pieces of furniture.

"You mean you're not even taking the old ice box?" I ask. He found it in a corner of the garage years ago and hauled it out. It had been painted a durable battleship-gray. What on earth are you going to do with that old thing, my mother wanted to know. He stripped all the paint away to reveal the beautiful old oak and the carvings in the front. It found a place in the dining room. She used to keep her pocketbooks in it, and their checkbooks. But there's no need for it out in California. We have plenty of storage space, my stepmother says. You take it.

Oh, I say. And I do. I've always liked it.

I take the organ that was in the den. I can give it to the mariners' chapel up at the seaport. I take the marble-topped dresser that my father picked up for five dollars when Victorian things were considered frumpy. My mother protested that one, too, but it stayed. I take the little secretary with glass doors and a drop-lid desk. I take my grandmother's Limoges china and her crystal from Sweden. I take the child's bed that she slept in when she was little, that my mother slept in when she was little, that I slept in when I was little, that my daughter slept in when she was little. I take the spinning wheel that my brothers and I used to pretend was a ship's wheel and we were sailors, and I take the wool winder that went with it. I take all my mother's table linens. I take her cookie tins and muffin pans and her potato masher. I take her beautiful crystal vases and the banana bowl and the antique soup tureen.

I take her silver tea service and all her silver trays. I take pictures off the walls.

Greg and I are really moving. I have to be back up at work by four o'clock. There is no time to waste. Back and forth, between the house and the truck. Finally we've just about done it. The house looks bare, and it sounds funny when you talk. Hollow. There are rectangles on the walls where pictures used to hang, lighter in color than the wallpaper surrounding them.

"I think that's about it," I say to my dad.

"Got everything you want, then?" he says, and puts his hand on my shoulder. And when he does that, a wave of sadness washes over me, and I want to run back out and unload the truck, bring all the things I have taken out of our house back inside where they belong. Why can't we stay here, and light a fire and have tea and talk and irritate one another and sleep in our beds when night falls like we used to and Grandad used to tap on the wall at bedtime and my daughter would tap back, their own secret code?

"Yeah, I think that's about it," is all I say.

THE BACK STAIRS

I WAS AFRAID TO ASK for things when I was little. I would go to the store with my mother and see something I wanted very much and not ask for it. It is odd that I felt that way, because my mother was generous with us. If she could afford it and it wasn't a harmful thing, I know she would have bought it for me, whatever it was. I think I knew it then, too. But I wouldn't ask. At Christmas, too, once I had figured out who Santa Claus was, I didn't have requests. I would look through the Sears catalogue and dream of things, but I was afraid to ask for them. I would hope for them, and I would try to arrange it so my mother could *see* me doing that, turning the pages and hoping, so that she would ask me "Do you like that?" and I would be able to say "Yes, I really do." But I didn't ask for things.

I think now that it was all about power. My mother was big and I was little. My mother had money and I didn't. My mother could choose to bestow or not to, and I didn't have that kind of power. And I hated my lack of power. To ask for something reminded me of it. And to risk having a request refused—that was an exposure of weakness I was unwilling to make.

The back stairs of the house where we lived were intended for servants to creep noiselessly up and down on, so as not to disturb the family by being seen on the main stairs. We didn't have any servants. My brothers thundered down the back stairs to the kitchen every morning, where they'd wolf down half a dozen eggs and a pound of bacon without even breathing hard. I used the back stairs, too, for imaginary romantic assignations with imaginary romantic heroes, for hiding from my brothers, for daydreaming.

I also used them as a place to cry in secret. When something hurt my feelings I would go there and cry in solitude. I would revel in the fact that nobody in the family knew I was there. It added additional pathos. They're going about their business as if I weren't here, I would whisper miserably to myself. A lot they care that their little sister is crying all alone in the back stairs. They don't even come to find out what's the matter.

Nobody used the back stairs much during the day—

just my mother, and then only if she happened to be bringing some laundry upstairs. So a little person could sit there and cry a good long time without anybody discovering her. More than long enough to work up a delicious sense of aggrievement. Or to get bored with the whole business, and go on outside again without anybody ever seeing.

It would be decades before I acquired any more skill than that at telling people what was bothering me or what I wanted. I became adept at convincing myself that the people to whom I refused to tell things didn't want to hear them. So my isolation could be their fault, sort of. Yet I continued to hope that they would understand magically, without my having to stoop so low as to tell them. If you really loved me, I thought, you would know how I feel.

What rot. People are so different from one another in the things they value, the things they long for. How on earth could one person know what another person was thinking unless he were told? But there are a lot of us around, people who assume that the ones we love will be able to read our minds. And who are angry when that turns out not to be the case. Or who are not ready to leave the moral high ground of our mistreatment just yet. It can be mystifying to be involved with one of us.

"What's the matter?"

"Nothing's the matter."

"Well, something's the matter. You're slamming doors and dashing around the kitchen."

"Just leave me alone, all right?"

This last is spoken in an accusing voice. That and the very public dashing around the kitchen are loud signals that something is amiss, but nobody is saying what it is.

Bad day at the office? Thinking about something sad? Something I've done? Something the kids have done? What is it?

Getting bored with one's own isolation is the best treatment for this. What has to happen is for those of us on the back stairs to realize, once again, that nobody's going to play twenty questions with us. If you want or need something, spit it out. If you don't get it, what have you lost? You didn't have it to begin with. And another thing—your request is only about *this thing*, this particular thing you want or need at this particular time. It's not about your whole life, and whether you're truly loved or not. So don't globalize it. Don't say, "Oh, that's right, just go ahead—don't think about me. It's always the same. It never matters how *I* feel." This is not never. Or always. This is just today.

These and other sensible instructions became the talking-to I learned to give myself in order to get off the back stairs. Of course, it won't work unless you really want to get off. That is not as simple as it might seem. It would be a mistake to underestimate just how perversely sweet a source of pride it can be to think oneself supremely and totally misunderstood and undervalued. It's not all that easy for many people to give it up. I'm not sure that misery really loves company. I think what misery loves is to be alone with itself. It's more miserable that way.

I was afraid to ask for things when I was little because I was afraid someone would tell me "no." And that if that happened, it meant that I was bad for having asked. And unloved. And weak, for having needed something. None of that was true, but I was afraid it was. To this day, I have to tell myself it's all right to ask for things. To this day, I would rather screw things up royally on my own than ask for the help I know I need. And, to this day, I require a talking-to to get beyond that. That's pretty amazing. It's been a long time.

NEVER TELL A KID SHE'S TIRED

MY GRANDDAUGHTER WENT TO BED each night at about seven o'clock when she was tiny. After those first awful months of not sleeping through the night, she became very regular in her habits, and at about seven o'clock or seven-thirty you began to see the end of Rosie's rope. Sometimes she would be with her grandmother and her aunt alone as this time approached, and I would watch her hopefully for signs of Bedtime Onset. I wanted to read the paper or do some writing or some other activity of which Rosie disapproved and which, therefore, you could do only when she was asleep. And sure enough, just before seven she'd begin to look a little desperate around the edges. Her play became slightly too frantic, her laugh just a bit hysterical, a little too ready to turn into a sob. Her eyes would grow heavy. You'd see more lid for a longer time when she blinked. She'd tug at her ear and pout, and when I would ask her if she wanted some milk, she'd start to cry a little and lift her arms so that I'd pick her up. And I did. I would fix her a nice bottle just right, and she would drink it while I stroked her tummy and told her she was the nicest baby in the world and her eyelids would droop further and longer and then she'd be gone.

One of the things I might say to her in the continuo of reassuring chatter with which I accompanied the evening fuss is "You're tired." Now when her aunt, a teenager, heard me say that, she would come running. "Don't *ever* do that," she'd scold. "*Don't* tell her she's tired. You used to tell me that and I hated it. It made me so mad. It's so mean." I didn't get it. "But—you *were* tired," I would say. Makes no difference, she'd tell me. She hated my telling her she was tired when she was little, even if it was obviously the truth. "You're tired" penetrated in a humiliating way the boundaries she was learning to erect around herself. It suggested I knew how she felt better than she did, and that was insulting. Part of being tired was being unable to recognize that that was what it was, and being told that infuriated a little girl who was already at the edge.

One of the jobs of a family is helping everybody develop these boundaries of the self. People need to feel themselves as separate beings, contained within themselves and responsible for themselves, not as Siamese twins or triplets or quadruplets with other family members. In our love for each other, we may intrude upon one another's boundaries in a well-meaning effort to "save" each other. Do a child's homework for him so he won't get an F; he's just overworked and overtired and it won't hurt this once. Insist on a play-by-play account of a teenager's telephone call—she needs to be kept out of trouble. Get in between two family members who have a feud, functioning as a distraction from what ails them. Families in trouble have a lot of this kind of thing going on: each member works very hard in undeclared ways at keeping the family afloat in an emotional sea that is rockier than anyone is willing to admit.

That kind of overinvolvement in each other is never a good thing. It never works in the direction of allowing each family member to find his or her direction in life. Each is too busy attending to the needs raised by the "rescuers" to learn who he really is. People need to be responsible for their own lives, and they need to be left alone enough so that they can learn to do that.

It is so hard, though, to leave one another alone. We have a struggle trying to figure out when it is good to intervene and when to hold back. We were given children who knew nothing, with instructions to teach them enough so that they could make their way in the world. When is it too much? When does our concern stop being love and become manipulation, whether we are talking about children or brothers and sisters or husbands and wives?

It is manipulation when it is indirect. People don't really get angry when you take a stand, but they do get angry, and justly so, when they find out you're trying to trick them into something. It is manipulation when it seeks to legislate feelings. You may have the right to demand a certain course of action, but they don't have to like it, and it is manipulative to demand that they do. Or to insist that they are not "really" feeling what they know good and well they *do* feel. Even if they are mistaken.

In families where indirectness has gone on so long that it's just part of normal life, a change to directness and honesty is accomplished painfully, and may feel like aggression or even cruelty. But in no other way can the young declare their independence from the old, the parents set their children free and taste freedom themselves. The creation of a self that can deal with the world demands that this occur.

The ancients told the story of Adam and Eve. When God found Adam and Eve in the garden, guiltily wearing their new aprons to hide their shame, they blamed each other in a way that diminished both of them. Who did this, God asked. Adam blamed Eve and Eve blamed the snake. Neither admitted to being a person with choices who had just made a bad one. But each was held responsible for his or her own choice anyhow, and each paid in his or her own way. That's the way it is. We don't make each other behave as we do. We are responsible for ourselves. I could put Rosie to bed. But I couldn't tell her she was tired. That's something she had to learn to tell herself.

♦

THE GIRLS

♦

WE VISIT VERA. She has just lost her husband after forty years of marriage. At the end, she had to change his diapers. He didn't know who she was anymore. She had to lift him in and out of bed. Vera is not quite five feet tall.

When my husband and I get to Vera's house, her friend is there. They worked together years ago. Today, after the funeral, they are reminiscing about old times. People they worked with, people who have been dead for years. They laugh at their own stories, these two elderly women. Vera's hair is thin and snow-white, and her voice is quavery. Her friend's eyesight is almost gone. "What was the name of the girl whose desk was on the other side of yours?" Vera asks. "Do you remember?" They talk on about a time before they knew what they know now. They were girls, then. They look at each other now, and they still are. Vera is the same person that she was in the forties. The pain she has just endured cannot separate her from what she was. I listen to them talk. I am grateful for their escape from the grim days just past.

My mother would be about Vera's age if she were still alive. She sometimes referred to her friends as "the girls." My brothers and I used to make fun of that; we'd point out that they were anything but girls, and she would laugh, too. But she didn't stop doing it. My mother and the girls were not vexed with the problem of what they were supposed to do and be. Sexual stereotyping, role models, consciousness raising—these things had yet to invade their afternoons. Their daughters' afternoons were different. One of the first things to go was the use of the word "girl" to refer to ourselves.

"I'll have my girl call your girl." Important men used to say that to each other. Some still do. I pictured powerful male lawyers in corner offices, staffed by girls. The girls looked like Maureen O'Sullivan, and they wore brief jungle costumes like the one she wore in the Tarzan movies. They called to each other over their typewriters, using the warbling yell that Maureen used in those movies to call Cheetah into the treehouse for supper.

The use of the word "girl" to refer to a female worker was eventually revealed as the put-down it was. It pasted a label that read "child" on a wage-earning adult, no matter how old she was, thereby insuring that she would see herself as subordinate and act accordingly.

I was talking on the telephone in my office when a salesman came in, wanting to see the business manager. I waved at him and pointed to a chair, indicating, I thought, that the man he wanted would be with him shortly. He was. I heard the salesman say something about having had to wait for "the girl" to get off the phone, and realized with a shock that he meant *me*. I still wish I had gone out there and told him off, but I didn't. It did start me thinking, though. I wasn't "the girl." I was the boss. But his careless remark stung me, and in a diabolical way, it made itself real: I *felt* young and irresponsible, absurdly guilty about talking on the phone while that man waited for someone else, as if I were not doing something I should have been doing. We girls feel that way rather easily. I don't think men do.

It is that kind of experience that has given the word "girl" a bad name. We now hesitate to use it at all. At a recent lunch with a young friend who is a high school student, I was struck by her reference to a chum (a *current* one) as a woman. I know what she's doing. She's asking me to respect her and her friend, and she knows that a girl does not command the respect that a woman does. But there was something jarring about it. Her friend isn't a woman—not yet. She's still a girl. Life is long, I thought, and life can be hard. Let's not grow up too quickly.

I'm not even sure I want to have done with being a girl myself. I remember the exhilaration of being on teams in gym class: "C'mon, girls, let's *go!*" the coach would shout, and we *went*. The extra burst of energy, the final sprint, the firm grasp of the relay baton as it passed from hand to young hand. No rings on those hands—not yet. We were girls, and the most important relationships in our lives were with each other. There was no fear greater than the fear that we might lose each other's friendship, no rivalry keener than that for best friend, no desolation greater than losing that place. We mystified and annoyed our parents with phone conversations beginning not five minutes after arriving home from school, where we'd been together all day. What could you possibly have to talk about, they wondered. Just stuff, we would say.

When grown women of two or three decades ago called each other girls, it was that feeling that they called back. Girls in school. Girls on teams. Girls together, in delightful conspiracy. Girls, who can whisper secrets to each other not intended for boys to hear. When women called each other girls, they defined themselves as they were before husbands and children and houses and in-laws and jobs encircled them. Before backaches and crow's-feet. Before the setting aside of dreams. It was not a neurotic trivialization of themselves. It was an affirmation of their history and their potential.

That's what a girl is: potential. She knows few limits. A girl is strong. She knows little of fatigue, only her own boundless energy. A girl is a comrade of other girls, all hard at the business of becoming. And when a woman calls herself a girl, she is saying that all of those things are still alive in her. There has been no sad break between what she was and what she has become. Or may yet become. The line of her selfhood is unbroken.

My husband and I leave Vera's house and start for home. Sometimes he calls me his girl. A Sensitive Male, he asks if I mind. I don't. I know what he is doing. It's the same thing Vera and her friend are doing. He is saying that my thicker waist, my laugh lines, my tiredness after a long day—none of these things hide me from him. He knows who I am, and who I have *been* is part of who I am. And he is my boyfriend, with his silvery hair, for if I am still the girl I was—somewhere—then he, too, carries his boyhood self within him. And so it goes. The years hurtle on. We both know what waits at the end of them. But it hasn't been so long at all since we were young.

My stepmother calls. "Hi, girl," she almost always says. To her, I really *am* a girl, the daughter of the man she married late in life, the only daughter she ever had. I sit down for a minute and we talk. She connects me with a slower world than the one through which I rush every day. She gives me advice: about children, about love, about worrying, about slowing down a little. She is a second mother to me, and it is good to be a girl again. No apologies. I'll be one. When I choose to be.

♦

FATHER'S DAY

♦

AS I SHOPPED for a Father's Day card to send to my father in California, I was thinking about his life now, since he moved out there, and how much it has changed. He is now really a man of leisure, puttering in his garden and walking his dog, taking a spin down to the coffee shop for a doughnut in mid-morning, dozing off in the afternoon if he feels like it. The careful attention given to his diet and his exercise routine and his medicine by his wife is a comfortable cocoon of love and humor in which he lives each day.

They got married when they were both old, and they don't take anything for granted like younger people sometimes do. But they don't panic over the brevity of life, either, at least not in their best moments. They just take it as it comes, acknowledging with regret the evidences of physical frailty as they appear and determining to live as well as possible for as long as possible and try to leave it at that.

People my father's age have learned, if they have attended well to what life has to teach them, that there are many things that they do not control. I am forty-one years younger than my father. Accordingly, I have not learned what life has to teach me about control as well as I wish I had, although I'm smarter about it than I was.

There was a time when it seemed to me that I had to control just about everything, particularly in the realm of relationships with people. I assumed, when I became a mother, that the kind of people my children would become was completely up to me. If I were a good mother, they would be good people. If I were a bad mother, they would be bad people. I really thought—and looking back now, I find it hard to believe I thought this but I did—that my children would *think* the way I did. That the things that were important to me would be important to them. That I would know everything about them, the way I knew when they were little everything they ate and everything they wore and everything they did. That I could mold them into the people I wanted them to be all by myself by my example and my words and the evidences of my love, and that everything they were and thought and did had everything to do with me.

I don't know how long I persisted in this delusion of

control but I do know that the adolescent years finished it off. Each child, in her own way, established her identity as a person separate from me, as I had to establish myself as separate from my parents. I didn't know that that was what was happening at the time, but I know it now. I thought, you see, as many people think when they are young, that there was a right way and a wrong way to parent a child and I knew which way I was going to use. I assumed, also, that my way would be superior in several important areas to the one my parents had used and that the results, therefore, were sure to be superior. Armed with an astonishing ignorance and a handful of old scores to settle, I was about as equipped to be a parent as I was to fly a plane: both were possible, but both would take some learning and some help. People who do important and difficult things like fly planes or raise children don't do them alone. They rely on other people. And they rely on circumstances beyond their control. The wind, for instance. The peer group, for instance. The airplane maintenance crew. The teachers at school. Luck. God.

For the person who has not yet grasped the truth of how little he controls, life is a series of manipulations performed upon the world and the people in it to make them do what he wants them to do. Life becomes a panicky affair, taking the most unpredictable creature ever created—the human being—and suggesting that it is my job and my right to control that creature. This is not about love. It's about power. The drive for power, which kills love more thoroughly than anything else I know about, *masquerades* as the love that is its victim, with phrases like "I am doing this for your own good" or "I feel so lonely when you're not around" or "If you really loved me, you wouldn't do things that upset me like this." The neurotic need for power puts me in between the people I love and their own destinies, suggesting to them that they should check with me first.

So when I slip into an inappropriate effort to control someone I love, I guess I must think I'm God. I guess I want to be that person's God. These efforts succeed just about as well as they deserve to, for me or anyone else, because we're not gods. We do not, even if we think we do, control other people. We do not even, in the end, control ourselves, for our lives are not in our own hands, and the control we do have and the decisions we do make about ourselves are all provisional. The inconceivable idea of our own deaths, the unthinkable idea that one day we will no longer live and the world will just close up the place where we were and tie it off and the people we think can't live without us are going to have to: in large measure, we don't control the time when that inconceivable idea becomes a reality. A hundred years from now. Or tomorrow, perhaps. The time will come for all of us when the will to survive will not save us, and we will die.

We all know about this. We all know we're going to die. But we don't all face death with the same serenity. I think we would like to get there before we die, though, to acquire that serenity before we are called upon to use it at the end, so that our deaths may be sorrowful and sad but not resentful. I have a feeling that the acknowledgment of our lack of control over things is the key to a serenity that can face death and accept it. I think we can, in a way, "practice" for our deaths by learning to achieve serenity in our lives. It was Leo Tolstoy who said that people die like they live, and he was right. If I have not given up my tendency to run things in life, how will I ever hand it over when it's time for me to die? If I act as if I thought I were God, what will I do when God dies? Who will be God then? What do you care, somebody might say—you'll be dead anyway. Well, yes—but the people who remain behind have only the testimony of the dying to teach them about death, since the dead are silent. What will my testimony be? Will I learn enough from life while I'm living it to see it as pure gift and surrender it gratefully, or will the pain of those who mourn me be worsened by the sight of me in a rage I didn't have to feel?

As I mailed my father his Father's Day card, I wondered, as I often wonder, how long he has to live. A long time, I hope, since he is so content in his life. But who knows? Who knows how long any of us have left? What can be done about it? Very little. But I am glad to see his serenity these days, and I remember that it was not always thus. And I am glad to see what serenity I have in me, and hope to keep it going and growing so that I'll have it when I need it. The day I die. And every day.

♦

UP TO WHITBY

♦

MY FATHER AND HIS FAMILY used to holiday with relatives in the ancient town of Whitby on the Yorkshire coast, a modest holiday befitting an impoverished clergyman's brood. I have always wanted to see Whitby. We had a little joke about it, my dad and me: he left a stuffed bear on the beach in Whitby when he was five, and he used to tell me I should go back and see if it was still there. At times, I have thought of the bear, waiting patiently in the sand, its button eyes scanning the horizon. Waiting for me to come and get it.

It *would* be a good place to take kids, I thought as our car breasted the cliff and we saw the North Sea for the first time. Nice beach. Whitby gazes watchfully out at the sea, scanning it for the Nordic invaders of centuries ago. Generations of Whitby men sailed the sea. The sea is wild and gray, and the cliffs were wild once, too, although now the lower ones sport nothing more menacing than a frumpy string of bed-and-breakfasts vying with one another for roomers.

The innkeepers haven't penetrated the highest cliff. They never will. On it is the ruin of Whitby Abbey. The abbey was the first thing a ship saw as it approached the coast from the north. Some of it stands today. You either reach it by winding up the steep cliff in a car as far as you can go and then walking, or by climbing the famous steps as people have done for thirteen centuries. We drove, arriving at the ruin just as the sun set. There were two reasons why I'd wanted to come all the way up to Whitby. One was to check on the bear and report back. The other was to see Whitby Abbey. Because of Saint Hilda.

Saint Hilda was a Celtic woman. She founded the abbey in the sixth century. It is said that she wielded tremendous power in the Celtic church, and exercised considerable secular power in the neighborhood as well. There don't seem to have been many serious differences between her authority and that which would have been exercised by a man in her position. Some say that there was a tradition of strong female leadership in the Celtic church, a legacy of pre-Christian practice. Whitby was the place where Celtic Christianity in England came to an official end and the more Roman Christianity of the Saxons took over. It happened after Hilda's time at the Synod of Whitby. From whom did your church get its authority, the king who presided at the synod wanted to know. From Saint John, answered the Celts. And yours? From Saint Peter, answered the Saxons. That was that—the king was not about to offend Saint Peter, who held the keys to heaven. The Celts lost the right to practice their rite independently and retired in defeat to Ireland, where they soon died off. So much for Hilda's church, with its special liturgies and its beautiful art. After ten years of dancing backward in the Episcopal church in America, the great-grandchild of Hilda's church, I wondered if she might not have a word or two of advice for me.

When I was first ordained a priest in the American church in 1980, the ordination of women to the priesthood was three years old. There weren't very many of us—fifty or so, out a total of more than ten thousand Episcopal clergy. The struggle leading to the women's ordination had been a painful one. It was believed by many that our presence would shatter the church, that Christianity as they knew it would cease to be. We seemed to them to be willful malcontents bent on ruining everything from the Sunday school to the nuclear family, or well-meaning but confused women who really didn't understand what was important in life, or women who had not come to terms with our femininity. People we had never met thought nothing of marching up to us to say that they didn't approve of us. It happened all the time. That seemed a sweeping statement to me. Approve of what? The fact of my birth? My behavior? My appearance? It was hard for women to get jobs. Few male rectors were willing to take on women as their assistants. They almost always blamed this on their congregations, who were "not ready." I used to wonder how they thought they would know when the people were ready.

I was lucky. I found a position right out of seminary. But scores of gifted women in those early years did not. There were few safe places for them to put the pain of that. We clung together to support one another. In my diocese we founded a club called WOE—Women Ordained Episcopal. We had funny meetings and parties to break the ice with the male clergy. We gave supporters purple T-shirts with WOE on the front. We seasoned the hard work with humor as best we could. But it was *very* hard work. We were acutely aware of the need to be upbeat and affirming, accepting insults with an understanding murmur and a friendly smile. Sometimes my face would hurt at the end of the day from all that smiling.

It didn't take very long for people to come around. Most people in the church got used to seeing women priests, and we no longer looked like freaks to them. Many people who had been fierce opponents became strong supporters. Usually the experience of seeing a woman do a decent job as a pastor was enough. But it soon became apparent that women would have a long and uphill climb in establishing themselves in positions other than as men's assistants. It wasn't easy, as time passed, to watch time and again as a man with less experience than a woman was preferred over her. But it happened all the time, and it still happens all the time. There is much less open rudeness. But we're not there yet.

I had gone to England to attend a conference. The

Church of England was struggling with the ordination of women, as my own church had ten years earlier. I went full of self-confidence. Certainly I could be of help. I had weathered the unpleasantness on our side of the Atlantic. This would be easier, I thought. After all, I'd done it before. All people need to see is that you don't have six legs, and they'll be fine. I gave an interview to someone in which I counseled people just to relax about it and not to panic. Everything would be all right.

I had forgotten, though, just how stinging a thing rejection is. I had come to feel that my self-confidence came from within myself, that it was something I carried with me. That turned out not to be the case—or, at least, it was not the whole truth. I had forgotten how important support from outside myself really was. And so I was horrified at the depth of my hurt when I was treated again in England as we had been treated a decade earlier in America, scolded again for ruining the church as if I'd done the awful deed singlehandedly. I guess I had forgotten how much those things hurt. Or hadn't dared admit it to myself at the time—too busy smiling. Or how important the fellowship of other women facing similar things had been in gathering strength. But it flooded back again, and I found myself fighting back tears at the most inopportune times. I learned—again—how needy we are for affirmation. That we don't bring it all with us—some of it has to come from other people. I learned how sweet a thing a kind word can be when an insult has found its deadly mark. I learned—again—that it's tough all over. I learned that from a wonderful man who told me the story of his rejection for ordination in the Church of England because of his divorce.

And from another wonderful man, a Welsh priest who opposed the ordination of women and feared for his church, but went out of his way to try and understand it. And from the laywomen at the conference, who lived daily with the general trivialization of women that seems to afflict the English in an offhandedly cruel combination of sexism and class consciousness. And from watching a group of male clerics respond with gusto to a degradingly suggestive performance by a young woman in a traveling French acting troupe, braying like drunken fraternity brothers, seemingly with no sense of this behavior being in any way inappropriate. And I guess it *wasn't* inappropriate, not there. Don't let the common language fool you, an English friend says. England and America are two very different cultures.

My head was full of these and many other images as the conference ended and I set off for Whitby. I was shaken by culture shock and surprised by anger, other people's and my own. I was ashamed of my tears. I felt weak and absurd and naive. I remembered with rueful clarity my self-confidence of only a week before. Now it looked like insufferable egotism.

The countryside grows wilder as one heads north. The moors are dark. The languid Oxbridge drawl disappears from conversation; the people all sound like my father, with their broad *A*'s and *O*'s. Their speech is imitated and ridiculed by people from other parts of England, like the speech of the deep South is likely to be imitated and ridiculed in other parts of the United States. I don't know how they feel about that when they travel around to other parts of the country, but Yorkshiremen certainly know who they are at home. There's something very fierce and stubborn about them, an openness about sharing their feelings with strangers that one does not find in the understated south.

The caretaker of Whitby Abbey had lived in Whitby all his life, he told us as we arrived at the ruin. He was walking around in it, doing a final check before closing for the evening. We were late, he said accusingly, but we could walk around with him as he closed up. We fell into step. He was tall and rangy and of indeterminate age. His stride was so long and he walked so fast that I had to run to keep up. I remembered running like that to keep up with my father, another tall, rangy man who talked like this one. We walked among the toppled stones and bits of wall. I said nothing about the church. I felt that I had said and heard quite enough about the church for one week, and decided not to offer any information about who I was and what I did for a living. Our host was eager to talk about it, though.

"Right there where you're standing—that's Hild's abbey."

"Right here?" I was standing on a hummock of grass. There wasn't a stone within fifteen feet of me.

"Under the ground. It's buried under the ground where you're standing. This that you see over here"—he gestured dismissively toward the ruined walls, "none of this was here then. It was built after she died."

"So Hilda's monastery is buried now."

"Not Hilda," he said angrily. "It's not Hilda. Her name was Hild. She was Celtic."

"Hild. I've never heard that."

"No, and you won't, either. People don't know that.

People don't know anything about her. She was the ruler here, though. She built this abbey."

"Yes."

"In those days the church knew what it was about. I'll tell you one thing: the church today is in ruins."

Here it comes, I thought. I was glad I hadn't blown my cover. That way I wouldn't have to pick up the tab for the destruction of the Celtic church along with my other ecclesiastical crimes.

He inveighed against the ruin of the church as we picked our way through the ruin of Whitby Abbey. Stone sarcophagi lay about haphazardly, as if discarded in a hasty resurrection. Each was startingly small, a reminder of the diminutive size of my Celtic ancestors. And each had a hole drilled in the bottom: a practical touch enabling the fluids of the decomposing body to return to the earth whence it had come. Ashes to ashes, I thought. Dust to dust. The empty shells of the dead. Hild. Her successors. The monks of Whitby Abbey. People who fought passionately for their church to be the way they thought it should be, fought as if life depended on it, dead and gone from the earth now, their coffins empty and clean as dry bones. And their issues dry bones, too, for the most part. Who today even remembers what the Synod of Whitby was? The church that supplanted the church of Saint Hilda has itself been supplanted, or at least it has been so tranformed that she would hardly recognize it as hers. People died defending it, but it was transformed anyway. And in the end, they all slept: those who longed to retain Celtic use and those who longed to stamp it out. Along with those who didn't care one way or the other.

My host wasn't making it very clear in what way the church was in ruins. I wondered if the ordination of women was part of the ruination for him. I didn't ask. But I would like to think that this man, who loved the very ground that covered the great monastery of Saint Hilda—sorry, Hild—would become able to see the inclusion of women in the priesthood as something of a piece with her. Something besides an outrage.

After the abbey was secured for the night, we said good-bye to him. He nodded gruffly and watched, silhouetted against the graying sky, as we began the careful drive back down the hill. He raised one hand in a farewell salute. Whitby Abbey, too, showed against the sky, dark masses of crumbling walls. Hild's abbey slept beneath the ground, hidden from view. Not a visible part of the church, but hidden, like I had hidden my priesthood from its caretaker.

We drove out of Whitby in silence. I asked myself why I cared so much what this man thought of me. I didn't know his name. I would never see him again. Why did I dread his disapproval, so much so that I didn't even tell him what I did for a living? Women priests probably *were* part of the decay of the church in his view, part of what he meant when he said that the church didn't stand for anything anymore. I was probably part of the problem as he saw it. And because I suspected that, I kept silent. Why?

I remembered the sight of him standing in the ruins, his square shoulders, his silent salute: one upraised hand. And I knew where I had seen it before. It was the way my father used to say good-bye, standing in the driveway as

I pulled away in my car. I would look back as I drove off and there he would be, one hand raised in farewell.

That man who had lived all his life in the home of my father's family reminded me of my dad. The same speech. The same walk. The same impatience. The same suspicion of the new. All my life I have wanted his approval. My feminism walked uncomfortably hand-in-hand with my desire to please him. My priesthood was like those good-news-bad-news jokes to him. He was proud, truly proud. But it was also true that my vocation was part of the new church in which he felt less and less at home. Other things became thinkable for the church because of it. If the church could learn from the political movement for the liberation of women, what other political movements might contribute *their* truths? Where would it end? Everything that my father was cried out to stand fast against change. And so much of what *I* was rolled right over him.

And he loved me. Enough to accept women as priests and learn to live with the ambiguity of that stance in view of his natural traditionalism. Enough to glow with pride when we officiated at services together. Enough, even, to consider his bishop a bit much because of his fanatical opposition to women in orders. We observe careful limits in our shoptalk. I have never discussed my views about the ordination of homosexuals or liberation theology with him, and I know I never will. I hide them. And, although he doubtless suspects where I stand and considers it morally repugnant, he lets me hide. It's not perfect. Some of my honesty must flower elsewhere. But my love flowers there.

What would it have been like for me if my father had

never left England? If I had grown up there? I think of my friend, a young woman from Essex who lives in New York now, where she can exercise her priesthood. She had to leave her home to do it. She lives half a world away from her parents, from her brother, from the farm on which her family has lived for generations. Will she go back when the Church of England opens its priesthood to women? She thinks about it. Probably not. It's very different there, she says. I'm really not part of that anymore.

What would it have been like if my father had never left England? I know what *he* would have been like: he would have been like the caretaker of Whitby Abbey. But what about me? How would I have approached my vocation if I had been an Englishwoman? It is possible that I might not have approached it at all. But he did leave. Left those cliffs, those dark moors, those familiar centuries behind. Half a world away. And here I am. What I am.

There was no bear on the beach at Whitby. I checked.

A KIND AND GENTLE MAN

SAINT PAUL'S CHAPEL is the oldest continuously used building in New York City. George Washington went to church at Saint Paul's. His square pew is still there, with his prayer book on a desk inside, and his comfortable chair. Our founding fathers—the Anglican ones, anyhow—believed in being comfortable at worship, so they brought in their own furniture for their family pews. They had curtains they could draw for privacy, in case the preacher went on a bit and they felt the need of a nap. Their servants, of course, sat upright for the entire service on the hard, straight pews in the center of the church, while their masters slept and chatted in the boxes that lined the walls.

Today Saint Paul's is a treasure of the city. A steady flow of tourists walks through all day, looking at the historical exhibits. Several times a week there is a free concert and the place is packed. There is a subscription concert series on Sunday afternoons. Once a month a famous writer comes and gives a reading. Sometimes plays are presented at Saint Paul's, and on Wednesday evenings in the summer there's a jazz concert for the after-work crowd. At lunchtime the walks and benches out in the churchyard are full of people enjoying a rare treat: a bit of green in lower Manhattan.

Every evening, a volunteer comes with a key to open the heavy iron gate to the churchyard. Several men are already waiting for her, and they follow her in when she has unlocked the church door with a second key. They turn on the lights, and begin making dinner in a makeshift kitchen underneath the stairs leading to the organ loft and gallery. Two of the men set up a long table in the back of the church, and begin to set it for the evening meal. Periodically, the phone rings twice and then stops, a signal that another man is waiting at the gate and needs to be let in. When all ten men are present or accounted for, the gate is locked for the last time.

These men are residents of Saint Paul's shelter. They sleep on cots in the organ loft, and they keep their belongings in metal chests at the foot of the cots. They rotate the housekeeping and cooking among themselves, and they have weekly meetings with a social worker, whose job it is to help them reenter normal life after having survived the trauma of their homelessness. A man must interview with the social worker privately and then with all the residents in order to be accepted into the community. He agrees to follow strict rules in order to stay. He knows that he can only stay a year from the day on which he enters, but he also knows that considerable effort will be put into helping him get on his feet during that time. Everyone who has managed to stay at Saint Paul's and work its program has found stable housing and employment, and is no longer homeless.

Everyone, that is, except for John Palko. John was one of the first clients when the shelter opened, and he lived there almost continuously until he died nine years later. He was older than the other men, although nobody knew exactly how much older, since John himself didn't know how old he was. My guess was early seventies, but he could have been a lot older. He didn't know where he was born, and he didn't know when. When John first came to the shelter he didn't talk at all. He would sit in silence in the group or at dinner. Late at night, though, he would sit up with Pat, who runs the shelter, and they would talk and smoke cigarettes. She was interested in his past, but she didn't press him on it. He seemed to have a hard time piecing it together. The parents' names he supplied didn't check out, and he said he didn't remember what had happened to them. He thought he was born in New Jersey, but he wasn't sure. Never been in the military. He'd gone to a lot of different places and done a lot of different things, but he couldn't always remember what they were. There was some question about the authenticity of his last name:

Palko. He might have been someone else once. The reason all this mattered was that you can't get Medicaid or Social Security if you can't prove who you are, and John couldn't. One time John was turned out of the drop-in center from which Saint Paul's drew its clients because he could not supply enough pedigree to get welfare, and Pat lost him for six months. She finally found him, sick and sleeping on the floor on the lowest level of Grand Central Station. She coaxed him back. And he never left again. The one-year-maximum rule was quietly forgotten. From that day until the day he died, Saint Paul's Chapel was John's home. He had no money. For all anybody really knew, he didn't even have a name. But he had a home.

He came in from Grand Central with the croupy cough that almost all homeless people have. After they've been sleeping in a dry place for a while, most people get rid of it. John never did. He grew a little stronger, but he still had that cough. Not that his smoking helped. Every night he would come slowly up the steps of Saint Paul's and slowly into the tiny sitting area under the stairs, where his old chair was waiting for him. It had been somebody's office chair once. It had a green leather seat, cracked and split, and the stuffing was beginning to ooze out of one corner. He would settle into the chair, being careful not to put his weight on the left arm, which had come loose from the frame. Then he'd light up a cigarette. That pretty much took care of his movements for the evening, except to come to the table for dinner. Mostly he just sat, the gentle Buddha of the shelter, listening to the conversation flow around him. Living in a secure setting for the first time, he became able to speak when spoken to, even to inquire after the health of a visitor. To laugh at jokes. To *tell* jokes, eventually.

Because John did *not* move on after a year—where was he going to go?—he became the patriarch of the shelter, the one who could remember how things had been done in 1984 or whenever, the guy who always knew where things were. He loved being the archivist of the shelter's daily life: he knew so little about his own. He began to talk in the group meetings, even to help settle things. The other men—younger than he—looked to him for guidance, and he showed a surprising ability to give it. And when a man moved on, he would often return from time to time to sit and visit with John, participating again in the community that had given him his life back. Sitting and talking into the night, while John smoked and told stories and laughed quietly at his own jokes, waving away concerned questions about his cough, men struggling to stay afloat in their newly rented rooms and real jobs got a shot of home, which kept them going for the week. It was like talking to my grandfather, said one of them. Because he never went away, John also came to symbolize the remarkable community of the shelter to the volunteers who came in and out of the men's lives every evening. There he was in his chair. Every night.

He told Pat that he thought he may have had an accident or an illness or something. He couldn't remember things. Couldn't remember his own parents. He couldn't remember the Second World War. Not a darned thing about it, he said, think of that. He formed the habit of looking things up in the library, so he could manufacture his own memories. He was in the library every day, researching his place in our common past. As a result, he was knowledgeable about a wide variety of subjects. He could talk about them as if he remembered them. Monty was a seminary student and a volunteer at the shelter; he slept over a couple of nights a month. John and Monty used to sit up at night and talk about the St. Louis Browns. They'd reminisce about famous games, players they both remembered. John told Pat later that he'd researched it all. Didn't remember a thing. Not sure he'd ever *been* in St. Louis. Funny, wasn't it, to be living in a place like Saint Paul's, such a historical place, when he couldn't remember so many things about his own life. It could have been from drinking when he was younger, Pat says. Or from something that happened to him that was too fearful to remember.

During the week, the men clear out by eight o'clock in the morning, so that concerts and services and tours can happen. This is just one of many reminders: they sleep at Saint Paul's, but it is not their home. Sunday is a sabbath, though, a day of rest for them as well, and they can sleep in and stay home all day. One Sunday Pat wanted the *Times*, and John offered to go and get one. She gave him a dollar. Off he went, and he was gone for quite a while. Came back with the newspaper *and* the dollar. He hadn't been able to find a deli that had one left, he said, and when he saw a guy carrying the paper he asked him where he could get one. The guy gave him his. And so he came back with the dollar that he could have kept without Pat or anyone else ever knowing. And here was John, with no money at all. But he was like that, Pat says. He was a good man.

People began to notice that John wasn't looking well in the fall. Volunteers began asking Pat about him. Sometimes she would have to let him stay up in the organ loft all day, even on a weekday, because he was too weak to go out. One day the security man came upon John with his arms around the refrigerator, his chest pressed up against it, trying to breathe. We can't have this, the man said. One of these days we're going to go up there and find him dead.

John didn't want to go to the doctor. He knew he'd have to go to the hospital. He knew he had emphysema. And he knew he was dying. And he wanted to die at Saint Paul's, the only home he could remember ever having had. That wasn't too much to ask. But, in the end, he had to go.

Saint Vincent's treated John for free, and treated him as well as if he had been a private patient. He liked all the nurses, and they liked him. They fussed over one another: you'll get bedsores if you don't let me turn you and rub your back, they'd say. You'll hurt yourself turning me over, he'd fret back, I'm too heavy for you. But he grew weaker. Soon, a ventilator breathed for him. Pat began to think about funeral arrangements. But then John seemed to rally, got off the machine, looked like he was making progress. Looked like he would go home after all. Great. But to what? Could a sick old man go home to Saint Paul's Chapel and live in an organ loft? Rules could be bent, but that wasn't going to fly. John wasn't going to be able to die at home like he wanted. He was going to have to go into a nursing home. And so, suddenly and surprisingly, in view of how well he'd been doing, John died right there in the hospital. He never had to face not going home.

They had the funeral service in Saint Paul's, of course. All the men came to the service, and many former residents came as well. All the volunteers were there. Several of the priests came. The cat who shares the shelter with the men was there. They took John's old chair, with its broken left arm and worn-out seat, and they set it up at the crossing of the church, up in front of the congregation. Pat sat in the front row, being the closest thing to family that John had. Monty the seminarian preached the sermon from the oldest continuously used pulpit in the oldest continuously used building in New York City. The sermon was about summer nights at Saint Paul's, John in his chair, Monty on the steps, talking about baseball games of the forties. It was about John's shadowy past, and his gracious presence in the shelter for all those years. It was about home, and what it means. And what it is not to have one. And then to have one.

The City of New York does not permit new in-ground burials south of 15th Street anymore. So they buried the broken left arm of John's chair in the cemetery of Saint Paul's Chapel, where three centuries of New York's great and near-great sleep. They used a serving spoon from the shelter kitchen to dig the hole. So now a piece of John's old chair is out there in the churchyard of the place he called home. His body is buried in Queens, near where Pat lives. A volunteer paid for the burial, and others chipped in for the tombstone. Since nobody knew his date of birth, they just used the day he died. And the only other thing they really knew for sure about him.

JOHN PALKO
OCTOBER 13, 1990
A KIND AND GENTLE MAN

I BRAG TO MY FRIEND ABOUT BAKING MY OWN BREAD

I BAKE MY OWN BREAD. It is the whole wheat, good-for-you kind, salt-free and leavened only by a sourdough starter. The starter is at least seven years old, and it is sort of immortal. You're supposed to use it fairly often to keep it alive and interested. If you don't bake with it for a week or so, then you have to give it a teaspoon of sugar for a snack. But it's really pretty rugged: I've taken it out of the refrigerator after a month of neglect, looking like the worst sort of rotted leftover you'd ever want to see, and in a hour or so it will be plump and bubbly and ready for anything.

I make sure my best friend knows when I am baking. This is because she doesn't bake herself. So I bring it up with elaborate casualness when we talk on the phone, telling her whether or not I've put cornmeal in it this time, whether the loaves are round or baguette. She always says something coarse about what I can do with my bread. I press on, gushing over the way it fills the house with its lovely smell, the way my dear ones love it hot from the oven. She tells me I make her want to throw up.

Both she and I work all the time, from too early in the morning until too late at night. Our corners are not dusted very often, and we don't fold our laundry anymore. But I retreat from time to time into a little nest of domesticity, baking things and sewing things, and from my nests I throw little commercials about homemaking at her that would make Martha Stewart blush. She catches them neatly and throws them back.

"So what's up?"

"Oh, I just put four loaves of bread in the oven. Richard *does* adore it, and it seems like such a little thing to do for my dear ones. And what are you doing, darling?"

"I'm drinking alone."

We both love this, and I'm not sure why. My unctuous one-upmanship cartoons the superwomen we both half feel we should be. Perhaps by cartooning them, we can leave their demands behind. We are aware of the inroads work has made on our lives. When my older daughter was little, I made apple pie. I made it a lot. Once, a few years ago, I heard my younger daughter tell a friend she'd never seen one made from scratch. I felt indicted. When had that kind of thing stopped?

I feel this more than my friend does. I am the one who indulges in the bread-baking orgies. And the sewing. And, once in a blue moon, the enormous family meals. And then calls her up to brag about these things, so that together we can lampoon them. A part of me wishes that life were made of only those things. As I race from meeting to train to meeting, the rhythm of the home seems like a holy peace, a serene continuum for which I yearn. But do not yearn for enough, apparently, to stay there for very long at any one time.

My friend did more time at home than I did, so she's less sentimental about these things. Because she put in that time, she seems less compromised than I am, as if she had a diploma I lacked. One that reads REAL MOTHER. Never mind that she didn't bake her own bread when she was home. Or that sewing was never her thing. She reminds me repeatedly that she stayed home to be with her kids, not to be the best baker in town. As she says this, I remember the anxiety with which I made the homeward journey at the end of a day, the longing—a physical one—to see my girls' faces and hear their voices. Reporting in sick when it was really one of them who was sick, afraid that my employer would find out. And then not being able to take a sick day when I *was* ill. Today, that behavior sounds like something out of the Stone Age. Were things really that hard then, or did I just make them hard? I really don't think I did. Those were the days when mention of something like maternity leave would have seemed as sensible as a proposal for free Sanskrit lessons, the days when people really did say things to women with children about getting out of the kitchen if we couldn't take the heat. And nobody thought they were out of line. We just bled inwardly, as we demonstrated just what terrific little heat-takers we could be.

My daughter is now a mother herself. She works, too. Just as hard as I did. She seems much less conflicted about it than I was—than I am—so maybe we've made some progress after all. And her younger sister, whose feminist credentials are somewhat more untried, can't imagine staying home all the time. Is so glad I didn't. But she doesn't know about the gut-level good feeling a mother gets seeing her children eat. Or how hard I had to work to get that feeling. Or to go along on those school trips. Or how I felt when I couldn't go.

Women balancing homes and jobs are nothing new. But we still beat ourselves up about it sometimes. And each other, sometimes. Both kinds of mothers—those who work outside the home and those who do not—are acutely aware that the multiplication of possibilities for women is a good-news-bad-news kind of gift. It has introduced ambiguities where certainties used to reign, and ambiguities are hard work. Among other things, they make people want to defend the choices they have made by claiming absolute moral status for them. Or by claiming that they were the only choices possible.

But we should take ourselves more seriously as moral agents than that. My choices were not forced on me. I made them. I *did* have to work when my children were young, but I also loved to work. And probably would have even if I hadn't needed to. I could have been a more passive worker, but I chose not to be. Like almost all the mothers I know, I did the best I could. Like almost all the mothers I know, I was often torn between the world of work and the world of home. I still am. But I don't conclude from this that there shouldn't be two worlds. If we don't take responsibility for the choices we have already made, we cut ourselves off from those we have the power to make in the future.

I sit in my sewing room, thinking about whether or not I'll retire early. Then I could sew all the time. I'm annoyed because I have to leave for a meeting and haven't finished the skirt I thought I'd have plenty of time to do. And who knows when I'll get back to it—could be weeks. Months, even. On another day, I sit at my desk, annoyed because someone at home needs me and I haven't finished the sermon I thought I'd have plenty of time for. It's the same feeling. My friend calls.

"What're you doing?"

"Writing a sermon and cursing under my breath. How about you?"

"I just did the most incredible group—incredible. I'm on my way to work out for an hour, and then I've got two individuals and then I'm seeing outpatients until ten o'clock. You wouldn't believe how incredibly rewarding it is."

"Aren't we the busy little bee."

♦

MEN ARE VERY DELICATE

♦

I THINK I HAVE TO FIRE A MAN. I have tried warnings and changes in the job description and other changes in the work location and God knows what else. But it has become clear that he has no intention of working at the level of excellence of which he is capable and which his colleagues maintain, that he may be less than candid in his reporting of the work he does do, and that his fellow employees see all this and are wondering how long it's going to go on. So do my superiors, who also, then, wonder about *me*.

He has had detractors for years. People have been telling on this guy ever since I became his supervisor. I have suspected that some of the snitching is racist, and I still think that. I have suspected that some of the misgivings I myself have had about his work may be racist, too, the impatience of a WASP who hits the ground running with a person of another, more leisurely culture, one that was producing masterpieces of literature and sculpture when my ancestors were sitting around a campfire painting themselves blue. But dammit, I say to myself, *I* didn't paint myself blue, and he didn't write those poems. We're just trying to do a job here, and I don't think he's trying very hard. I have kept him on too long for the good of the group already.

He has a wife and two children. Can I put a father out of his job? When should I do it? Before Christmas so his unemployment can start the first of January? Or should I let him get through the holidays in innocence? What if he argues with me? What if he begs me to keep him on? What if he hates me? What if he drew my name for the office Christmas party?

I have known for a long time that one of my biggest enemies is my own desire to make men feel good. I threw spelling bees so that boys could win them. I remember one that I did not throw, and I am *still* cut by the hate in the glance Patrick Reeves shot me thirty years ago as I spelled "foreign" correctly and won. I have felt responsible for men's inadequacies all my life, it seems, and have expended a fair amount of energy shoring them up, patching them together so well that the stitches barely show. I have felt responsible for helping them to conceal the areas in which they fall short, creating distractions from these unpleasantnesses by serving as a loud cheerleader for the smallest of their virtues.

This makes me a very kind boss. I love everything they do. If I don't love it, I feel it's somehow my fault. In a way that I now think emasculating, I have wanted to pick up after them, cleaning up their messes, following them with an invisible whisk broom and dust pan into which I sweep their mistakes so that nobody else will see them. In doing this, I deny them the opportunity to learn from the consequences of their errors, the painful but educational road people have to travel to advance. I have to fight myself—hard—to avoid showing these hurtful kindnesses.

I am not alone in this. Generations of women have made sure men looked smart and strong. And have made sure *they* didn't appear too smart and strong in the presence of the Other Kind. The male ego, we were told, simply couldn't tolerate the threat. It was only recently that we gave ourselves political permission to stop doing this. At last, we said, we can be what we are. What shocked me —continues to shock me—is how reflexive a thing it is for me, still, to try and smooth their paths. I still feel an obligation to support men in their work.

I type for a colleague when something has to get finished and all the secretaries are up to their ears. I made my living as a secretary once upon a time, and I'm fast. He uses a slow hunt-and-peck. I offer to help, and am proud of my speed. I love him. And I feel happy to have helped him meet his deadline. But I am also aware that what I have just done is a very stereotypical thing. I've put aside my work to help him finish his. I'll get mine done somehow. I always do.

Why aren't there more famous women composers and rocket scientists? One reason is that men are usually the ones who decide who's going to be famous. The other one is that men can usually find women to help arrange their worlds so they can do their work. Nobody does that for us. Men are encouraged from childhood to be singleminded about their work, not to allow any distractions. And women are encouraged from childhood to set things up for them so that they don't have any. Don't make so much noise; your father is working. And when do we do *our* work? Late at night, when everyone is sleeping. Or early in the morning, before anyone else is up.

As a result of being spared like this, men have a low threshold for distraction. They are *delicate*. They are made nervous by having to do more than one thing at a time. They feel frazzled and angry if they have to answer three phone calls, and have a hard time settling back to work after the trauma. Women, on the other hand, develop the skill of doing many things at once. They tuck the phone in between their shoulders and their ears, hold a baby on one hip, stir a pot on the stove, all the while thinking about an idea for a story. They don't think it's unfair to have to do this. They think it's normal.

Women are just more complex than men about work. We've learned how to be that way. We've learned to love our ambidextrousness, our snatches of solitary time, and to make the most of them. For years I got up at five so I could write with no kids around. The kids are grown up now, but I still do that. It has become my most creative time. I wouldn't give it up for anything. It's not particularly fair that it was necessary, but there you are. Men do their jobs brilliantly when they have little else to do. I should think they would. If they contended with the additional jobs many women have, they'd measure success differently. And they'd be stronger.

The goddess Kali, friend of Hindu women, is depicted with nine arms. That's about how many you need. She's not as affirming to men as we tend to be; she rains down death and destruction on those who treat women unjustly, and she doesn't care who they are. I don't know about *that.* There's got to be a middle ground between our colluding in men's privileging themselves and wanting to kill them. Marrying later may help—more brides today go into marriage with established careers and work habits than used to be the case. They have negotiating skills that ought to help them get a fair shake. Their husbands carry their babies around in canvas slings and shop at the same time. That's progress. But even now, even with babies in slings, the burden of home and child care is not equitably distributed in most marriages.

But it's an imperfect world. Things usually *aren't* equitable. Somebody usually has to give. It's usually the woman, and it usually makes her mad if she has time to think about it, and then she usually gets over being mad and makes the best of it. And grows in complexity as a result. Life is short, and most people don't want to fight their way through it. So couples point out to each other from time to time that things aren't fair, and a fairness that fits is found. It may be a little lopsided, and it's irritating when people pretend it's perfectly symmetrical. It's not. But it fits. That's the important thing.

♦

SHOWING OFF

♦

I AM MOVING INTO THE CITY. The loft apartment into which my husband and I are trying to fit everything is sleek and modern, with track lighting and important architectural details. Our furniture is going to look a little strange in here, I can tell already. But we'll think about that later. Right now I'm unpacking boxes.

I open one. It has not been unpacked since the *last* move. I have no real use for its contents. They are the linens I've inherited from my mother. And from my grandmother.

And even a few from my great-grandmother. A snowy white linen tablecloth edged with a crust of handmade lace. A pair of round doilies, delicate as spiderwebs. Blanket covers with tatted edges and more tatting down each side, where the edge of the bed would be. Lace that has become with age the color of café au lait, and lace that has been retired from its original use, cut away from a dresser scarf too threadbare to use, retrieved from the cuffs of a dress no longer worn. Plain white towels bordered with Swedish embroidery, wedding gifts to my grandmother from her friends.

The homes of these women were beautified by these things: simple household objects embellished for no other reason than to delight the eye. And, although I don't have a use for most of these treasures, I feel as connected to them as if they were family photographs. At the turn of century there was the flash of a metal crochet hook, in and out, in and out, a thousandfold. A *thousand* thousandfold. And then there was a frost of lace spread out on a table. And then there was a satisfied nod as my great-grandmother accepted her own work: a long and narrow lace runner for a table or a dresser in her newlywed daughter's first home. I never knew her. She died before I was born. Her daughter is dead, too, and *her* daughter is dead. But I am alive, and I feel her achievement as I pull the lace she made into shape with my fingers. I know how she felt at that moment. "There!" she said. "There!" I say to myself as I finish writing something and know that it is good. "There!" we say, as we finish decorating the church for Christmas and step back to admire our work. "There!" as the actors deliver their last lines and the lights go down, leaving them and the audience in darkness, aching with pleasure at what they have just shared. "There!" as bread comes from the oven a perfect brown, smelling like heaven itself.

The joy of creating beauty is something women have always known about. When their lives were more limited than women's lives are now, there was always a way to adorn the necessary with a grace beyond function. That there was pain involved in that flowering of creativity because of the places it could *not* go only adds poignancy to what it produced. And there *was* pain. Our foremothers lived circumscribed lives in comparison with ours. And yet they made what beauty they could with what they had. And it was beautiful indeed.

And there was pain. I think of Mary Cassatt, the American painter who went to live in Paris, where her art could breathe more freely than it could in her native land. Childless, and a defier of many conventions, she nonetheless returned again and again to studies of mothers and children on canvas. These are the paintings for which she is best known. At first glance, in their quiet domestic settings or in their beautiful gardens, they are all icons of maternal peace. But look more closely: in many of the paintings, something is wrong. The mothers seem not to be on the same plane as their children, or to be holding them a little uncomfortably, or not to be looking at the same thing. They look into the middle distance with oddly empty expressions on their faces as their babies twist on their laps. They are beautiful. The gardens are beautiful, and the light and the colors are beautiful. But something is just the smallest bit off.

What Mary Cassatt is showing us with her uncomfortable madonnas is the dividedness of her own soul with regard to the life she has chosen: the tug-of-war between the longing for motherhood and the longing for selfhood. To pursue her art she closed certain doors in her life. She knew that what lay behind them was profoundly absorbing. In these paintings, she looks wistfully behind these doors. And from the canvas, her subjects look wistfully back. At what *they* have left behind. There is sweetness—and darkness—in that which binds us forever to our children.

What Cassatt suggests in oils is made stormily explicit in prose by the favorite aunt of our girlhood, Louisa May Alcott. Her heroines have to *choose*, and they are anguished by their choosing: Love or Art. Not both. The strong-willed hoydens of Alcott novels put aside their dreams for domesticity and its embroideries, and the author commends this womanly choice. At book's end they are honorable, happy women, but they are profoundly *not* their old boisterous selves. Something new and beautiful has been added, but only because something else has been taken away. And in some of the *unpublished* works of this unmarried booster of hearth and home, the dreams of art and writing win out instead, and those heroines see and taste the delectable fruit of their genius. But Alcott could not create a heroine able to encompass love and art together. There are only happy mothers whose brushes and palettes collect dust, or solitary artists whose joy is found in what they create. Women in relation to others or artists alone. Not both.

Fanny Mendelssohn. Clara Schumann. Both composers, like their famous kin, but we have only recently come to know them well. Jane Austen, shyly publishing her first novel, *Sense and Sensibility*, its authorship ascribed only to "A Lady." Subsequent novels were written "By the Author of *Sense and Sensibility*." None of the editions published during her lifetime bore her name. Her gravestone in Winchester Cathedral, placed there by her grieving family—"They Know their Loss to be Irreparable," it says—makes no mention of her writing. They knew about their own loss, but were silent on the world's loss of a genius who died young. They mourned their sister, daughter, aunt—but Jane Austen the writer was as anonymous in death as she had been in life.

Most women writers of her era handled their authorship in the same way. They knew—or felt they knew—what the market would bear in the way of women working openly in creative arenas defined and claimed by men. And so the public display of their art was characterized by a profound diffidence, as if public acknowledgment of their work were not something to which they should aspire.

Many of us know that feeling. Many of us have a sense that displaying our creativity is somehow "showing off" and hence inappropriate. That the most worthy work is work that is unsung. Or many of us have been exasperated by that feeling in a woman we love and whose gifts we admire: "You really should publish this!" we cry, only to hear "Oh, I couldn't do *that!*" as a response. We are safe if our art is securely a hobby. We are less so if we expose it to the weight of public scrutiny. And so much of the work of women, even now, is under wraps, or enters the public arena by the back door of avocation. As different as our world is from that of Louisa May Alcott or Jane Austen, we know about the feeling that makes us keep our work at arm's length from ourselves. Sometimes we just don't sign it. Even now.

I think of my great-grandmother. "There!" she said as she spread out her lace. I say the same thing when I have written something I like. But my name is right there in black and white, while it is only because my mother told me that I know who made that incredible lace. I am so glad that I know.

THE TOMBS OF THE MEDICI

THE ARNO HAS SMELLED AWFUL since we got here. I am not one of your Americans who carries a can of disinfectant in her purse to use in public toilets. I worked on the waterfront for seven years, and I know what a river smells like. But Florence this week smells like something died in the basement. Maybe I'm just tired.

I *am* tired. I do not visit the Uffizi. I will decide later whether or not to tell anybody I didn't visit the Uffizi. Instead, I find a P. D. James I haven't read and curl up on the loggia of our hotel for a good read. Even my husband the enthusiast is tired. He, too, does not visit the Uffizi. He sits with me and writes letters. By evening, we both feel better. We go out for a walk. Soon we reach the Church of San Lorenzo, and we step inside to have a look at the Medici Chapels.

Expensive. The tombs of the Medici make a statement. "We're richer than you are" is what they say. The Medici lie in sarcophagi shaped like Victorian bathtubs, made of green and white and gray marble, intricately pieced together. Where something can be embellished, it is. It is hard and cold in here. It is difficult to imagine someone mourning one of these guys. There is, of course, no sign of their wives. I believe they are downstairs somewhere. There is no sign at all of *anything* real connected with the lives of those whose bodies sleep in those marble tubs. Just some Michelangelo statues linking two of the Medici with virtues they may or may not have possessed. Fancy. But formulaic, like a ready-made greeting card, not personal. And very cold.

The Medici ruled Florence in somewhat the same way that Tammany Hall ruled New York. They were money people before they were political people, and there was no need to pretend that their rule had anything to do with anything except power. This sudden kind of power—Florence was next to nothing until it invented and funded the Renaissance—gave the whole society what New Yorkers would call an attitude. Even now, when the best of Florence is at least five hundred years old and precious little of value has been added since then, everyone has it. From the crabby woman who serves breakfast at the *pensione* to the students elbowing one another out of the way in the line at the cheese shop, Florence is a city of two-year-olds who all need naps.

That it was brilliant when it was brilliant—that's true. The place to go for the best this and the best that. A place where an artist could create cleanly, without having to clothe his work with theology if he didn't want to. A place where to be human was enough; no further justification of creative genius was needed or desired. The first Western painters and architects with names emerged here. To make the human the measure of the good—that was new. It freed the race from some shackles that needed to go. Like superstition. And the stunting of intellectual inquiry in the service of religious paranoia. It made it possible to rejoin the best thought and art of the ancient world, without having to dress it up in Christian clothes.

But, though it was free, it was not generous. It was selfish. It was not a movement intended to raise up the whole human family. Only rich people. It was not for everyone. It was only for them. This considerable new freedom seems not to have made them happier or more peaceable. All they did was commission artwork and beat each other up.

That is why there was Savonarola, a Dominican monk who came to Florence and was soon appalled by its excesses. And so he set himself to reforming it in the name of moral values, making his foreign provenance a virtue, like modern American presidential candidates sometimes brag about not being Washington insiders. He argued for the restoration of a genuinely republican form of government, one that would give the people a say in things. This would put the city back on a Christian course, he thought, and save it from the fires of hell. Art was part of the problem. People weren't thinking about God enough because things were too beautiful. It was distracting. A lot of it wasn't about the Bible. And it took money away from the poor. So he exhorted the people of Florence to gather up art treasures and books and make big bonfires of them in the Piazza della Signoria—the famous "bonfire of the vanities." Incredibly (I couldn't get them to make me a cup of *caffè latte*) the Florentines went along with this. But Savonarola's experiment with a religious republic didn't last. While people did want their currency revalued and their tax burden lifted, most of them didn't really want to be all that good. And they *liked* art. Besides, they missed the festivals and pageants the Medici used to put on for their enjoyment. Savonarola was burned at the stake himself a few years later, in the same spot where he had held his bonfire.

The Medici were never really the same after this. They continued to rule in Florence for a while, but there were other centers of power and culture more compelling, other rich people with power in other places, and a whole new half of the globe to contemplate. The intellectual and artistic excitement of fifteenth-century Florence gradually became a thing more to be curated than created. The best had already been. The final legacy of the Medici to Western culture was an inadvertent one: the Restoration figure of the Italian fop.

We leave San Lorenzo and come out into the late afternoon sunlight. It is still warm, and I realize that I was cold inside the Medici Chapels. We walk through the streets as it begins to get dark. The tombs were irritating, I tell my husband. So egotistical and cold. The Medici were irritating. People don't usually become rich and powerful because they're nice, my mate remarks. They didn't then, either. You have to take what's good and leave the rest.

That's what the world has done with the Medici. They were richer and stronger than anyone else, for a while. But now they are dead. And people stroll through their monuments, enjoying their art without them—people whom they certainly would not have chosen to entertain when they were alive. The power that the art celebrated is gone. Florence is not a capital of the twentieth-century world. And now only the artists are still alive for us. We have to look up their patrons' names in books even to know who they were.

LE HAMEAU

THE CHÂTEAU AT VERSAILLES is closed on Tuesdays, so we will not be seeing the Hall of Mirrors, or any of the rooms where the Bourbons danced and played billiards and conducted their famous intrigues. That's okay. The gardens are the most important thing at Versailles as far as we are concerned. My husband will go and take pictures of something he needs for the book he is writing about gardens in the eighteenth century. I will wait here for him, in the garden of the Petit Trianon.

The Petit Trianon is what it sounds like: a smaller version of the Grand Trianon, the house Louis XIV built for his mistress. During the reign of Louis XVI, the king's family used the Petit Trianon as a place to get away from the ornate oppressiveness of court life at Versailles. Marie Antoinette especially loved the Petit Trianon, which she visited daily. It was there that she tried to hide on the day the mob came from Paris to arrest her and her family.

Most of the gardens at Versailles are seventeenth-century and very formal, with orderly gravel paths and topiary trees and geometric plantings and very little shade. The purpose of the garden surrounding the château was to make a statement about the absolute power of the Sun King, and it does that. The garden is an extension of the palace; some areas of the garden, in fact, are called "rooms," as if they were not outside at all, but part of the house. Nature herself falls under the dominion of the king, these gardens say. She is trimmed, confined, and obedient. She is *not* wild.

Things are different at the Petit Trianon. The house is not imposing. It is small, and it is made of beautiful marble in a soft pink. Where the gardens of the main house are geometric, these appear to be natural, laid out at random. Winding paths disappear into inviting leafy glades where a person might sit and rest awhile. Enormous boulders in grotesque shapes hang over the path in a way that the landscape architect probably hoped looked Chinese. Walking along the path, I catch sight of a tiny temple—to Love, naturally—that looks as much like a Greek one as the eighteenth century could make it look.

I am the only person here. I haven't seen anyone else

in the garden at all. It is completely quiet. I realize that I don't even hear an unidentifiable mechanical hum. It is seldom completely quiet for modern people. There is usually a machine somewhere, doing whatever it does, and we are usually hearing the sound of a motor. These sounds are so much a part of our world that we are completely unaware of them, unless they suddenly stop. Then we look around for a moment, aware of a new silence. But here in the garden of the Petit Trianon it really is silent, as it was when the people for whom the garden was made walked and sat in it. I sit down on the grass under a tree and slip off my shoes. I dig my bare toes into the grass. I am not concerned about getting grass stains on my dress; it is a sensible cotton one from L.L. Bean, and you can do anything to it you want. I think of the confining clothes well-born women wore then, their stays, their tight bodices and sleeves, their large skirts, their panniers ballooning out on each hip. Hot in the summer. The men, too: tight silk stockings and tight breeches. Heavy coats. Lace at the neck. This new-fashioned garden must have been irresistible to those corseted people. So unlike the guarded paths of the rest of Versailles. A place to be free and wild in the midst of the careful minuet of court life.

At the far end of the garden is *le hameau*. It is sort of a theme park, an artificial French farming village with thatched roofs and little paddocks and a barn. Marie Antoinette and her friends used to go there and dress up like peasant women. Farm animals were kept there for their amusement, and they would play at being shepherdesses.

Marie Antoinette was not French. She was Austrian. She did not enjoy the stifling elegance of the Bourbon court, to which she had come as Louis's bride at an early age. And the court didn't like her much, either. Her early awkwardness in the French language came in for regular ridicule, and she made the mistake of showing that the presence of royal mistresses shocked her. People laughed about that for years. It is hard to know who she really was before tradition made her what we remember her as: the let-'em-eat-cake girl, symbol of everything that was wrong with the French monarchy. But she was just a young lady who was married off for the convenience of others and grew into a woman with not enough to occupy her time. There is no reason to think that she was any more callous in her disregard for the poor than anyone else in the aristocracy: her famous bon mot is probably either apocryphal or out of context. As for her husband, he seems to have been almost enlightened, as Bourbons went. Reading the democratic handwriting on the wall, he began a political response characterized by at least some intelligence and generosity of spirit. Too little, too late, though. The damage had been done by those who came before him.

This garden, and the artificial village in it: they are so unlike everything else at Versailles. *Un jardin anglais*, they called it, in an admission of English influence rare in France. The careful achievement of naturalness, the desire to make it seem that nature is unfettered, that the garden just *happened*, is the hallmark of the English garden as the French understood it.

I walk toward the little houses of *le hameau* and think of them romping there, running instead of walking, howling with laughter at their own ineptitude at herding sheep, their corsets and stockings off, their feet bare. In a few years, real peasants would be using some of these very gardens to grow potatoes. Or so the tradition says. And Marie and her ladies would be dead. And her husband. And her children. And their way of life.

Did they suspect that it couldn't go on? Is that why it suddenly seemed like fun to play at farming and tending sheep? Perhaps something in them knew that they were becoming obsolete, and so they began, purely in the realm of art and play, to experiment with a world that would be more inclusive than the one into which they had been born. The French had loved Ben Franklin when he visited the court a few years before. They regarded him as an oracle of rustic wisdom from the brave new political world across the sea. Swaddled in their brocades and perspiring in their wigs, they admired his simple clothes and plain hair. But they must also have seen that this simplicity represented a threat to the only way they knew how to be. Was there a way they could have it all? Could they be a part of the new world and still stay on top of the old one?

No way. Too much anger had been stored up for too long in the people upon whose backs they had lived their lives. Whether or not they could have reformed, whether the artistic beginnings of respect for the poor would ever have grown peacefully into genuine political partnership, it was not to be. There wasn't time for them to learn. And they couldn't have it both ways. So most of them died.

Revolution announces itself first in art. And fashion. The rich hope that they can somehow contain the desperation of the poor by admiring the artifacts of their daily lives. And, in our century, by buying them. My mailbox back home is being stuffed with half a dozen catalogues every day. Some of them sell the handicrafts of third-world people, the baskets and blankets woven by poor women in Honduras and Guatemala, set forth in a glossy booklet so that I will buy. And the advertiser makes sure I know that this is a project of this or that women's weaving cooperative, appealing to my sense of justice along with my interior decorating savvy. I can buy these things and help those poor people. Terrific—we both win. But I have had too great a head start for them ever to catch up. Americans are eager to buy these things, eager to display the beautiful baskets and rugs in their homes, *very* eager to hear about the weavers' cooperatives, eager to be a part of the free-enterprise system's healing balm on poverty's grinding ache. But that is as far as we go. We are not eager to hear that our being rich is intimately connected with their staying poor. Can't we just buy what they are selling and stay the way we are? It is unimaginable to us that a day could come when we are not on top anymore. It was unimaginable to the court of the Bourbons, too. But it happened.

Marie Antoinette frolicking with her sheep in *le hameau* has seemed to later generations to be the embodiment of decadence. Rich people playing at being poor people. But was it really just ridicule? Wasn't it the same unwitting foresight we display when we appropriate the arts and crafts of the poor for our living rooms? Marie has become, for history, the Leona Helmsley of the eighteenth century, the extension into absurdity of an entire age's greed. Leona, in fact, also kept sheep on her estate in Connecticut. She thought they looked nice on the grounds, and she enjoyed making a fuss over them in front of people. And when she grew tired of them, she had them butchered into chops.

I leave *le hameau* and walk along the path, heading back toward the house. I hear the sound of somebody running toward me on the path, but I can't see him. There are too many twists and turns. Why is he running? I am suddenly frightened, for I have seen no one at all since I arrived, and it is getting on toward dusk. The great rocks seem more menacing than they were when I walked past them earlier. I stifle an urge to hide behind one of them, and force myself to walk naturally. The runner is getting nearer. Then I hear a shout. I am flooded with relief when I recognize my husband's voice.

He shows me the place where Marie Antoinette is said to have hidden in the rocks and mud on October 5, 1789, listening for the first shouts of the mob as they searched for her. I think of her crouching there, hearing her own heart pound with fear. And of the young page who ran along the path looking for her that day, coming to tell her that the people had reached Versailles.

THE PEARL

ONE OF THE BOOKS on my daughter's summer reading list was *The Pearl*, by John Steinbeck. It lay around the house all summer, and one afternoon I picked it up. I'd forgotten how good it is. I was a young person myself when I read it the first time. But now it seems to be about people I know.

The story concerns Kino, a young fisherman, his wife, Juana, and their baby son, Coyotito. They live in an unnamed place—maybe Mexico—where people fish for pearls. Kino, like all the other men, hopes to find the perfect pearl, one that will be so large and so beautiful that it will make his fortune and assure his family's prosperity. As the story begins, his hope is an urgent need: the baby is ill, the gringo doctor won't treat him without cash, and Kino doesn't have any. So he dives down into the water to the oyster bed to try and get a pearl. He sees an old oyster in an out-of-the-way crevice, untouched for years, and pries it loose and brings it up to the boat, where Juana and Coyotito wait. He opens the oyster and there it is: the pearl. Larger than anyone in the village has ever seen. White like the moon. Perfect and lustrous. Kino's heart sings. He'll be able to save his son. He'll be prosperous.

The pearl changes Kino's life. And Juana's. And, most of all, Coyotito's. Word gets out about the pearl, and someone wants to steal it. Kino and his little family flee the village and take the pearl up into the mountain caves to keep it safe. They are pursued. And there in the caves, in his struggle to keep the pearl, Kino loses just about everything. The thieves shoot randomly into the caves, and one of the bullets strikes Coyotito in the head, killing him instantly.

That's all. The book is short—it's a novella, really. The next-to-the-last image we see is Kino, walking down the mountain from the cave. He is followed by Juana, who carries a stiff little bundle wrapped in a bloody blanket. And the last image we see is Kino and Juana throwing the perfect pearl back into the water. It gleams on the sea bottom for a moment and then disappears forever into the mud.

I remember when I was thirteen and read that last

paragraph. How sad I was about the baby and the young parents. I don't think I was angry, though; if I was, it was only at the thieves. And at the doctor. But I reread it as an adult, and as a person who works among poor people, and I am filled with anger on their behalf. Why was Kino willing to leave his home for the pearl? Why was he willing to fight for it and face danger for it, and put his family in danger for it, risking his life and theirs? It was because he was poor. Because he had nothing and lived among people who had nothing. It was because he needed to care for his family and couldn't because he had nothing.

I think of the thousands of seafarers I have known. The great ships that carry cargo all over the world are crewed by people like Kino. The officers may be first-world maritime academy graduates, but the crewmen are usually poor people. I've visited more than four thousand of their vessels, and I know. They go far from the people they love for a year at a time, with no furlough. Sometimes longer. They can go for months at a time without knowing whether the people they love are alive or dead. They risk their lives, and sometimes they lose their lives. Seafaring is dangerous work. They endure insult and racism on board, and suspicion when they are ashore. Sometimes their companies get into financial trouble and just don't pay them, hoping they will be too dumb or too discouraged to fight for what is rightfully theirs.

Why do they do this? Americans with lots of choices in life often ask me this question: Well, if they don't like it at sea, why don't they do something else? After all, nobody's *making* them go. What well-fed nonsense. Why do they do it? Because they're poor. Because they've had double-digit unemployment and triple-digit inflation at home for years, and there are no jobs for them. Because they need to provide for their families and can't do it any other way. And so they scrape together a thousand dollars from their relatives and friends and they buy a job illegally and they go off. And sometimes they don't come back.

And they sacrifice, in a sense, the very thing for which they went to sea. So that their families may eat, their children go fatherless. A man leaves a toddler and returns to a four-year-old who looks suspiciously up at him from behind his mother's skirts. He doesn't know who I am, the father thinks. I am only a photograph to my own son. And on board, treated, often, like machines, they begin to feel like machines. Lonely, they feel the distance widen between themselves and those for whose sake they work. Will my children know me? Does my wife still love me? Do I even still love *her*—do I love anything anymore? Can I remember, here in the belly of this great steel ship, what it is to love?

One of the things we help seafarers do for themselves is to fight back legally when their rights are being violated. It is not easy to assert oneself in a foreign country where the laws are unfamiliar. No wonder they hang back. They know that mounting this kind of a fight may get them in serious trouble back home. Americans today have the sense that the right to join a union is practically in the Bill of Rights, but there are countries in which it's against the law to organize labor or to litigate in a foreign court. Putting up a fight when a contract has been violated can be a dangerous thing for a seafarer to do, and he can feel acutely alone. But the chaplains are people he knows he can trust.

And they have a lawyer expert in seafarers' rights who can be reached at any time of the day or night. Doug tells them what they can try, what might work for them and what won't. If they need to retain counsel, he helps them do it. And if there's nothing that can be done, he tells them that, too. Sometimes it's not worth the risk. Sometimes a man knows he would win such a fight and elects not to pursue it because of fear of reprisal at home. I can't go further, he says. I've got a wife and children at home, and I can't lose my license or risk going to jail. But even then, even if it is only by trying every possible means of helping to no avail, the chaplain tells the seafarer that we respect them as the skilled workers they are.

That is why poverty is more than an unfortunate fact of life. It is an injustice. As long as people are beaten down, they are willing to grasp at anything in their need, and they are willing to sacrifice things they shouldn't sacrifice, and they are willing to be treated in ways they shouldn't be treated. And others benefit from that willingness.

I am dusting a shelf. I come upon a picture, which an Indian seafarer made for me by gluing straw onto a piece of cardboard. It shows a fishing village—like Kino's—with palm trees and little houses, all made of straw. On the back he has written his name and address, so that I can come and see him if I am ever in Vishakhapatnam. His address is as follows: "Behind Sukanya Cinema in Gopala Patnam". It is very small, he explains. We don't have house numbers. It isn't really a house. It is against the fence. Behind the cinema is enough. Anyone there will know me.

I look at the strange address. The man lives in a lean-to in the street. I have two addresses myself: one in the city and another in the country. We each live where we live by accident of birth. I was born in a country that colonizes countries like the one he was born in. I have two homes and he lives in a shack. Yes, I know that there are poor people here and rich people in India. And that I have worked hard for what I have. But he works hard, too. While I have done nothing myself to make him poor, I know that we are both part of a system that depends on the continued poverty of some to assure the continued prosperity of others. And that I am one of the others. I can stay with my family and support them. He had to leave his at home, behind the cinema in Gopala Patnam.

TROUBLE LOVE

KOKO IS A GORILLA. She lives in California with an anthropologist named Penny and a male gorilla named Michael. Penny hopes that Koko and Michael will have babies together someday. Mother gorillas in captivity, though, don't seem to do very well by their children. They neglect or even hurt them. They won't nurse them. Penny is hoping to counter this difficulty by teaching Koko some mothering skills before the blessed event. She invites human mothers to come and visit with Koko, nursing their babies in front of her so she can see how it's done. She shows her pictures of mothers taking good care of their children. And she talks to her a lot about mothering. This is not as useless an exercise as it sounds, for Penny has also taught Koko to communicate in American sign language, the language of the deaf. Koko has a vocabulary of about a thousand words—about like that of a two-year-old human child. She knows how to ask for what she wants by name. She can order from a menu. She can describe her feelings and render opinions. She can ask questions.

Every so often, Koko is in the newspaper or featured on a radio news broadcast. An animal that can talk. She was on the cover of *National Geographic* a few years ago, a great black ape, cradling a tiny kitten in her enormous leathery hand. The kitten was a gift from Penny. Koko had asked for it—signing "love cat," getting excited over pictures of cats in her picture books—"love that." The first offering had been a stuffed cat—no good. She wanted a real one. Then a friend's cat had a litter, and Koko was allowed to choose a kitten for her own. She chose one without a tail. And she also chose his name. She called him "All Ball." She carried Ball around with her, tucked in her thigh, like a gorilla baby. She tried to make him nurse, as she had seen the human babies do. She let the kitten walk and climb all over her, and even let him bite her, without retaliating—although she would usually sign "obnoxious" when he did it. She brushed his fur, and frequently examined his eyes and ears for parasites. Once she found ear mites, and brought the condition to Penny's attention. She tried to dress Ball up in doll clothes. She was supremely happy. "Koko love Ball," she said. And she found motherhood a strain sometimes, too, just as we do. "Trouble," she signed about Ball one day. "Trouble." And then, "Love."

Talking with Penny, Koko struggled to put her love into words. "Soft good cat cat," she signed. "Soft good cat cat." Tell us about your cat, Koko. Well, he's—I can't find the words to describe how it feels when I cuddle him against me—*soft*. But so much more than soft. And good—how can I tell you about the feeling I get when we play? Just good, that's all—but that's not nearly the word. I don't know the word. And what about "cat cat"? Sounds like human baby-talk: "kitty-kat." I wonder if that's what she meant.

In this clumsy effusion of praise, I recognize all who love. Mothers. Children. Lovers. What is unleashed in the soul when we love is sharp. We do not expect it. We didn't know we could love so wildly. It is beyond words, yet it demands to be communicated. We don't do much better at finding words for it than Koko does—our floweriest attempts fail to convey the depths to which we are stirred. Don't even begin to show what it is we mean. We give up. "I love you," we say helplessly, over and over. We can't get any more specific. We don't have the words. We do it about as well as a gorilla speaks English.

My kids and I fell in love with Koko and Ball. We came across a picture of them cuddling and put it up on the front of the refrigerator. We began calling all three of our cats "soft good cat cats." And then one night, listening to the radio in bed, I heard the announcer say that Ball had been killed. He ran out in front of a car. I sat up in bed, unable to believe what I was hearing. It was as if a member of my family had died. Of all the cats filleted on the nation's highways every day, why *this* cat? This cat, whose unself-conscious play and soft little body had stirred deep love in the heart of the great ape, love that pushed her to share it in her passionate, clumsy speech. Love that blurred the distinction between animal and human. Is this being, who can turn to a friend and grope for words to describe her love, an animal? Because if she is, then so am I.

I looked in the *Times* the next day. There it was. Koko did not see the accident—Ball was found dead on the road by someone else. When Penny told her what had happened, Koko made no answer at all. And she went and curled up in the corner of her trailer. And she wouldn't eat. And she wouldn't talk. For a long time. Then she cried. After a while she began to talk about her grief with Penny: "Cry, sad, frown." "Blind, sleep cat."

I think the motherhood lessons were a success. Koko, who had only herself to worry about, opened her heart to her kitten, and thus became someone whose heart could break. That is the other shocking thing we learn from love: not only how wild a thing it is inside me, but how easily my heart can be broken. It's easy to hurt me. Just take my love away. That's how you can hurt me. No wonder there are people who would rather not get into it. Love is dangerous if you do it right. As Koko the gorilla now knows. I don't think she will neglect her baby, if she has one. She knows how to love something small.

I don't know what plans are being made for a pregnancy attempt. Koko's not getting any younger. Michael will need to be brought on board, of course. In the meantime, Koko has asked for and gotten another cat. A cat with no tail, like Ball. This one is orange. She named it Lipstick.

♦

SOME OF US ARE NOT ALLOWED TO DIE

♦

THE MOTHER OF Ferdinand Marcos, ousted president of the Philippines, died a few years before her son did. Like the rest of the Marcos family, she had achieved during her lifetime a degree of fame that made every event in her life a matter of intense public interest. The mother of the president was revered by a people who find it easy to get worked up over singers, movie stars, and sports heroes. Her famous son knew very well just how to work this national enthusiasm to his advantage.

That is why, when the elder Mrs.

Marcos died after Ferdinand Marcos fled the country in disgrace, the supporters of the Marcos regime who remained behind in the Philippines could not find it in their hearts to bury her in the normal way. With the flair for the dramatic that characterizes much of Filipino politics, they had her embalmed and then just left her out. They would bury her, they said, when her son could come back and do it right—so I guess there was something more going on in the veneration of Mrs. Marcos's mortal remains than simple respect for the dead. Last I knew of this she still lay in state at one of the Marcos country homes, which had become a magnet for pilgrims from all over the Philippines. A funeral director comes from Manila once a month to inject the body with embalming fluid, so that Mama would retain her good looks. Thousands of people have visited the body. Miracles are reported to have occurred at the site.

The body of Vladimir Ilyich Lenin, the founding father of Russian communism who landed on top when the dust of revolution cleared, has lain in state for public view a lot longer than the elder Mrs. Marcos—more than fifty years longer. The party faithful can go and have a look at the architect of their political life any time, even though he has been dead all these years. Now that they've decided to jettison the system Lenin founded, the lines are long at his tomb. People want a last look before he finally becomes one with the earth, which ought to be any time now.

Everyone interesting who has died in Paris, from Molière to Gertrude Stein, is buried in Père-Lachaise, the eccentric Parisian city of the dead. Their monuments outdo one another in creativity. But at the corners of many alleyways a single word is scrawled in chalk: "Jim." An arrow points the pilgrim in the direction of the grave of Jim Morrison, lead singer of the Doors, whose driving rhythms and darkly suggestive lyrics sang the clenched fist of a generation. His image—the flowing dark hair, those burning eyes staring straight into yours—hung on dormitory walls all over the country, right next to the Day-Glo ones about love and peace, suggesting that love and peace were not the only things in the air during those years. Morrison died of a drug overdose about twenty years ago, and all the anger and the energy that leapt out of those eyes at us died with him. Following the trail at Père-Lachaise, one comes upon Morrison's grave. A nothing-much stone marks it. Pilgrims who are too young to remember Morrison sit on the ground and on other stones around the grave, passing around joints and bottles of wine, taking pictures of the grave, playing Doors music on portable tape players. The mood is festive. This is because many of Morrison's fans believe him still to be alive and living somewhere else. Graffiti on a neighboring stone sum up this dissent on what we think we see at Père-Lachaise: "What the fuck are you doin' here? Jim's not in there. Not a bone." Yet this grave—where he is not—is a sacred place.

The veneration of the bodies of the saints became a feature of Christian life at a very early time in the history of the church, so that pieces of them were sprinkled all through Europe and the Near East by the fifth century A.D. A toe here, a knuckle there, and legbone or a skull somewhere else—some of the saints seem to have had somewhat more than the usual number of body parts, so that if you were to put them back together from all the relics that claim authenticity, some of them would walk a little funny.

It's not only love that does this. Sometimes we need the dead to stick around for us to hate. Adolf Hitler is a name that our century has come to use as a synonym for evil. He put a bullet through his head in a bunker in Berlin, leaving instructions to his aides to burn his remains after he had done so. The man who destroyed so many lives and maimed the heart of a great nation was dead.

But very soon, people began to say that he was not dead at all. He was alive. He had been seen in Argentina, or in Colombia. The maniacal fires of his hatred still burned and still threatened a world that already reeled with the knowledge of what he had lately done. For forty years an occasional headline in the supermarket has trumpeted the news that Adolf Hitler is still alive, still dangerous, even though, if he *were* still alive, he would now be an old man, more than a hundred years old.

So we praise famous men—and famous women—and for us they live forever. But we are not ourselves famous men and women. Our own deaths are not beyond imagination at all, and when we allow ourselves to think about death, or about death touching someone we love, we grow pale with the certainty of it, and we push it from our minds. Our uniqueness as people who love and work, who are connected with other people in ways that matter—we hold on to this specialness in the face of the great separation we know is to come. They cannot die—they are part of us.

And so Elvis is sighted in Hawaii. He is living there with Marilyn. Jim Morrison writes his music now under some other name. He doesn't answer his phone. You can shake your head at such goings on—saints with six legs apiece, the poor old stuffed lady in the Philippines, whose body could not rest in peace because her son's supporters could not accept the reality of the end of his era, the kids at a rock star's grave who swear up and down that he's not dead. But we all know firsthand about the strong feelings we have for the physical bodies of those we love. A small lock of hair that I cut from my mother's head when she died lies in a little silver box on my dressing table still. When she died, I found myself wearing some of her clothes in those first few days, as if my walking around in the clothes she had walked around in somehow made her death less final. I remember a little girl who had lost her father; she insisted that she be allowed to sleep in one of his old undershirts that first hard night. That which had surrounded his body surrounded hers, and it was a little like being held.

It is hard to let go of the body. It is the only way in which we know how to be together. The fact of our imprisonment in the world of time, where the minutes tick off on watches and clocks, where days are crossed off calendars and years rung in and out, where youth runs out the door without a backward glance—that world of time is a physical world and we love it physically. With our bodies. We love it mightily. We don't want to lose it—not any of it. And so there are some people who are too important to us to die. There are some people whose lives seem so tied up in the ongoingness of our lives—sometimes because we know and love them, more often because of what they symbolize to our culture—that we cannot bring ourselves to believe that so random a thing as death could pluck them from among us. It cannot be that they, too, like anybody else, fall under the jurisdiction of death. So we just don't let them. We need them too much to let them go. And so we whistle in the dark. People tell one another that they are not dead at all. They are still alive.

RACHEL AND HER MOTHER

TWO YEARS AGO Rachel had the lead in the school play. It was *Forty-Second Street*, and she tapped up a storm. Everybody said she was really good. She *is* a good dancer, and carries herself like one. She's been dancing since she was four.

Brenda is Rachel's mother. She is a drug addict. She has been one for as long as Rachel can remember. Rachel does not know who her father was. Her mother gives different accounts of him at different times. She tells Rachel he is dead. Rachel thinks she probably just didn't know who it was. But she's not sure. Maybe she really did know, and maybe he really *is* dead.

Rachel does all the cooking—what cooking there is. They eat a lot of frozen food. She does the shopping. She does most of the cleaning. She goes and sits in the emergency room when her mother overdoses, and helps her get home when she is released. Brenda hurls abuse at her about being lazy. But Rachel manages to get herself to school most days. She doesn't always do very well. There is nobody to check her homework or to see that she gets to bed at a decent hour. But she goes. And she's almost made it through high school. Rachel is a senior this year.

Brenda has tried to get straight a few times, but it never lasts. She goes to a rehab for a few weeks. Then she comes out again, and stays off drugs for a few more. Rachel and her friends refer to her behavior at these times as "being normal"; Brenda talks and cleans the house and even cooks a little. Rachel laughs with her friends about these times; Brenda's making Jell-O again, she says. They laugh with her. They are very cool about Brenda. It's no big deal. They think of their own mothers, with their tuna casseroles. Rachel comes right home from school when Brenda is being normal, to spend time with her. Brenda and Rachel talk about how maybe Brenda should try and get a job. Rachel says encouraging things to her mother, pretending that a world waits eagerly for Brenda to decide to enter the job market. But she knows that Brenda has no job skills, and few friends who are not also addicts. There's not all that much she can do besides get high. She's very good at that. So she always goes back on drugs.

In her way, Brenda loves Rachel. She worries that

something bad will happen to her. She can't face the fact that she herself is already something bad happening to Rachel. She is not capable of much interaction, but she sits and watches television with her daughter and her friends for as long as she can. Then she makes an excuse to go down in the basement, where she shoots up, and then she sits down there for a long time in the dark, crouched against the wall. Rachel usually just lets her sit. At least she's quiet. Then when the drug wears off, Brenda is nervous and fretful, pacing around the house. Anything will set her off. Rachel tries to get out of the house when Brenda is coming off a hit.

Rachel has come to accept the fact that her mother has no control over her own actions. Getting high is the important thing in her life, and it comes first. So it is not easy for Rachel to see that her mother loves her. Or, at least, that it makes any difference that she does. Brenda often tells Rachel what a hard life she has had. Rachel tells me she wishes that *just once* her mother would realize that it's been no picnic for her, either. But she never does.

Somewhere along the line Brenda got hooked up with Frank. Frank has a lot of money. For a long time they lived together. Rachel, Brenda, and Frank. Moved out to the suburbs into a beautiful house in a nice neighborhood. Rachel has gone to the same high school now since ninth grade, the longest she's ever gone to the same school in her whole chaotic life. But Frank has finally gotten fed up with Brenda's drugging, and he's moved back into the city. Alone. Now it's just Rachel and Brenda again. And Rachel realizes that there is going to be no money coming in at all, and that Brenda isn't going to do anything about it.

Rachel has kept in touch with Frank. He is a decent guy. He told her that he'd help her out so she could finish school, but that he can no longer deal with her mother. Rachel can understand that. She can't deal with her anymore, either. And now their lease is up, and Brenda cannot pay the rent. They're going to be evicted. She has sold everything in the house for money to buy drugs. Rachel came upon her a few weeks ago, unplugging the little television set in Rachel's bedroom. I've got to get high, she explained, and walked out the door with it. Rachel decided it was time to leave.

Rachel has found an apartment. Frank will pay for it. Brenda will not know about it. Rachel and her girlfriends go shopping for some furniture and dishes. They have fun picking things out. Everybody is excited about the new place. There are two bedrooms. They're big. They will all spend the night with Rachel on weekends. They are envious, these young women who are soon to leave home themselves. Next year, they will all be on their own. But Rachel has a place of her own *now*. They go home from Rachel's apartment to their houses, where their parents want to know where they've been and did they have a good time and have they got all their books together for tomorrow. Their parents are annoying.

Rachel comes up the stairs and fumbles for her keys. She opens the door of her apartment and finds that it is just as she left it this morning before school. Her orange-juice glass is on the table. She forgot to turn the radio off. There is nobody home.

Rachel gets out her math book. She is actually on the honor roll this term—first time ever. She is applying to colleges. She hopes she'll get in. Being a dancer should help, I tell her. They look at things like that. When she was little, she remembers, she used to go to dancing lessons after school and she and Brenda would come home to an apartment like this in the city. Somewhere along the line, Brenda saw to it that she had lessons. Given her condition most of the time, that was no mean feat.

Rachel remembers what it was like learning to dance, being noticed and admired by other people. What it was like learning to turn on the tips of her toes. And then coming home to the apartment with Brenda, just the two of them. She wonders where her mother is right now, and if she's all right. Except for the radio, the apartment is quiet. She switches it off, and wishes things were different.

FEET OF CLAY

I RECEIVED A TELEPHONE CALL at a dinner party on a Saturday night. Who could it be, I wondered, as I made my way to the phone. One of my daughters must be ill. Or my granddaughter's fever must have gotten worse. There's been an accident, maybe. Or something has happened to my father.

It was my colleague. "Did you know you had the seven o'clock service tonight?" he asked. I looked at my watch. It was after eight. I looked around at the other guests and the nice food and searched my memory for this little piece of information. No, I hadn't known. I checked the little blue datebook that I use instead of a brain and it wasn't written down in there, either. The party had made it into the book, but not the seven o'clock service. I hadn't known I was on duty, although it had been in black and white on the schedule I received weeks in advance, which was somewhere in the turmoil of my mailbox and which, incredibly, I had not seen. No, I hadn't known. The only people who knew were the thirty or so people who came to church to find it dark and without a priest and who, after a while, just said a few prayers and went on home. Never in my years of ministry had I missed a service. Just not shown up. It was too late to do anything about it now, of course. We stayed a half hour longer at the party and then went home.

At home, out of the public eye, my reaction to the knowledge of what I had done was extreme. I was furious with myself and deeply ashamed. I cried and shouted and, if you can believe this, *banged my fists* on the countertop. The next morning they were black and blue and hurt like hell. It's a good thing the only other person there was my husband, who loves me, because it must have been a dreadful sight. I tried, of course, to find someone else to blame, to see if I couldn't find a way that this might be someone else's fault, but I didn't get very far. In my rage at myself, this failure seemed to me to cancel out eight years of service in that parish, to have wiped out every good thing that my ministry had ever been. I have seldom, in my life, been as unhappy as I was that night, and I have had some unhappy times in my life.

Exhausted, I went to bed. And the next morning, analyzing my extreme behavior of the night before, I realized that what was really bothering me was that I absolutely *cannot stand* being wrong.

Now, I don't know anyone who *enjoys* being wrong. We are not built that way. And most people, when they suspect that they are wrong, have steps they take to conceal that fact from themselves and others: finding someone else to blame, or minimizing the failure's effects. But we are all *going* to be in the wrong from time to time, whether we like it or not, and we had better get used to it and accept it in ourselves. It's dangerous not to. I could have broken a hand.

In the ancient church, people sometimes delayed baptism until they were close to death because they did not want to sin after they were washed clean. That way, they would enter the next life with no black marks. They felt that getting baptized and washed clean of sin and then sinning *again* put them in a bad position, so they waited until the last minute, when most of the really good opportunities for sin were gone. I can understand that. In my monumentally ungracious behavior when confronted with my own mistake, I would have done anything for it not to have happened. I didn't want to have done it, and yet I had. I didn't want to have a sin. But the next day, as I looked at the violence with which I dealt with myself over my sin—and in the scheme of things, how hideous a crime was it, after all?—I saw that this fascination with my own virtue was itself less than virtuous. It was pretty bad. It made my self-love conditional upon my own good behavior, and it paralyzed me. I was so angry at myself, I wouldn't have been able to commend the good that is in Mother

Teresa of Calcutta had she walked in the door. Hating myself, I could love no one.

If I thought that my life was valid because I was perfect, I should have been disabused of *that* heresy long before that night. And I didn't think that. I *had* a pretty good idea of what my shortcomings were, and I knew that I had some a lot more serious than missing a service. I just didn't want anybody *else* to know about them. It was their exposure that night that hurt; now thirty other people knew about one of them, too.

The next day I preached a funny sermon about this incident. In it I apologized to the folks who had come out for the service the night before, and told them I owed them one. They laughed. I showed them the black-and-blue marks on my hands and described how I had gotten them, and they laughed again. Maybe a little less heartily. I told them that it is good to have one's faults unambiguously revealed from time to time, in order that one may know wherein it is that we are acceptable. It is not in our perfection that we are loved. It is in the honest confession of our imperfection. Our clear conscience does not come from our assurance that we have not sinned. It comes from our assurance that we are forgiveable. That is what I told them.

TED WHO HAS AIDS

THIS IS THE THIRD TIME Ted has been in the hospital. Once when he was diagnosed and twice with PCP—pneumocystic pneumonia, rare in the general population but common among AIDS patients. We all carry this virus in our lungs for our whole lives and never get sick, but people with AIDS can die from it, having no way to fight it off.

Ted is used to hospitals. He worked as an orderly in one for years. Not the one he's in now, another one. "I don't see the people from work anymore. I've been gone so long. You know how it is. People are busy." Ted doesn't really mind that too much. He's half afraid to see someone from his old life anyway. He doesn't know how they would react if they knew he had been HIV positive when they worked side by side. "I was on AZT the whole time, from the moment I knew. But people are sensitive about it," he says. That's an extremely charitable way of putting it, I think. They sure are, I say. Do his parents know?

"My parents are both dead. I'm actually just as glad. This would kill them anyway. I was brought up Baptist—very strict. I never told them . . . they would never have been able to accept the fact that I was gay. I know they wouldn't have. And now this . . ." His voice trails off and he looks out the window. Then he looks at me again. "They were fine people," he says softly.

He misses his mother especially. Ted has a coterie of lady friends, older women who fuss over him and mother him. He loves that. He loves to chat with them, loves it when they plump his pillow and smooth his sheets. He tells them they are angels. And they love him, too. They hold his hand and fuss at him about eating more. They put wet cloths on his forehead when he spikes fevers and bring him cold sodas and pieces of fruit.

But they are not there all the time. The days are long for Ted, and the nights are longer. A bad case of shingles—another fringe benefit of the disease—makes it almost impossible for him to sleep. He asks for a sleeping pill. But I feel so terrible the next morning when I take it, he says. It gives me terrible dreams. He awakens drenched in sweat.

"The worst thing about this is not being clean. I'm an

extremely clean person. I worked in a hospital, you know. I can't stand the way I am now." Ted has almost constant diarrhea. Often an attack is so sudden that the nurse cannot get there with the bedpan fast enough, and he soils himself. And then he lies there in his own liquid excrement until somebody can come and help him.

"Did you see my roommate over by the door?" Ted asks me in a low voice. "He's famous. He was with the Alvin Ailey dance company." I stop to say hello to the man on my way out. He is tall and beautifully made. His skin is golden brown and his eyes are the same golden brown. His hospital gown and his sheets and his legs are covered with shit. His genitals are exposed and he is too weak to care. He looks at me in silent misery. "I'm so sorry this is happening to you. I'll get the nurse right away," I say, and I go and find her.

Ted says he thinks that he may be being punished for being gay. One of his lady friends is a fundamentalist, and that's what she told him. She wants him to repent so he can go to heaven. I tell him I don't think that's how God does things. I tell him I think God made him the way he is and doesn't punish people for being what they are. I point out that babies get AIDS, too, and they didn't do anything wrong. Oddly, he rejects my words in favor of hers. "She's right, you know. It says it right there in the Bible. What I did was a sin, and I'm paying for it now."

My blood runs cold. I want to find this woman and give her a piece of my mind. And I don't understand Ted. Why does he listen to this stuff? Maybe he's like the man on his deathbed who was asked if he renounced the devil and all his works. "Listen," the man said, "in my position I can't afford to offend anybody." Maybe Ted is hedging his bets in his last days, listening to me tell him what I want him to believe, his fundamentalist friend tell him what *she* wants him to believe, anybody at all tell him what the truth is so Ted can keep all his bases covered.

Or maybe he just misses his mother. And with her fresh fruit, her soft, tender hands, her hellfire and damnation, this lady is the most like her of all of us.

Tomorrow Ted is going home. He has a little apartment near the Brooklyn Bridge. His disability income just covers his rent and Con Ed. Medicaid takes care of his medical bills. He gets a meal at noon from God's Love We Deliver, a group whose mission is to bring nourishing food to homebound people with AIDS. They never turn anybody away. The meal Ted gets is huge—more than he can eat. He can save some of it for dinner. So he has a roof and lights and food. But the phone company is threatening to cut off his phone. Ted is in a panic. What if he needs an ambulance in the middle of the night and can't get one? He's afraid of being alone and getting sick. I could die and nobody would know, he says. I negotiate a deal with the phone company and send them enough to keep them quiet for a while. I ask them to call me before they cut Ted off. I tell them he hasn't long to live.

He has longer than I think. He spends the winter at home, mostly. One more trip to the hospital, once when he was too weak to breathe. But he got better and came home again. There's a church in Brooklyn—not a hellfire one, this time, but an Episcopal congregation—that has sort of adopted Ted and taken over a lot of his day-to-day headaches. Someone drops in every day to be sure he is all right and to clean up around the place a bit. The Baptist lady with repentance on her mind calls regularly, a counterbalance to the Episcopalians. Every once in a while the phone company calls me, and I send them some hush money. And Ted calls me himself.

"Mother Crafton, is that you?

"Hey, is that you, Ted? How's it going?"

"I'm hangin' in. I have a favor to ask. I need a coat. It's so cold outside."

"Well, you don't *go* outside, do you, Ted?"

"Well, I think I might pretty soon. And I don't have a coat to wear. Can you get me one, please?"

I don't really see the need for a coat. The man can barely arise from his bed. But people often give me old clothes, and pretty soon somebody comes along with a man's coat in good condition. So I put it aside for Ted. One thing leads to another and I get busy. The coat sits on a chair in my office for a long time. One day a homeless man comes in, wearing only a thin jacket against the January cold. I give him Ted's coat. I'll get another one for Ted. I still don't see the need for it myself.

"I really need that coat."

"Are you going outside, Ted?"

"Well, not just yet. But I think I will be soon." So I find another coat and take it there. Ted is a skeleton. He looks like a survivor of Auschwitz. He cannot walk. It is clear that he will not be going outside again. But he is grateful for the coat. It has been so cold, he says. It sure has, I say. I fix a cup of tea for Ted and another for myself. He drinks his from a straw, a tiny bit at a time. We talk a little bit about his old life: What was good in it and what wasn't. What he misses. He laughs a little. I was pretty crazy back then, he says, as if it were a century ago. He thinks a lot about whether he may have infected someone else. Or maybe more than one. I hope I didn't, he says. I wouldn't want anyone else to go through this because of me. Not ever.

He gets tired when he tries to talk, he says, but he likes to have company. The people at the church have been so good. Somebody comes over every day. He likes to have people around. He has a Bible beside his bed. I look at it and wonder if his Baptist lady gave it to him so he could look up his sins. I surprise myself, being so hard on this woman I've never even seen. I read Ted the Twenty-third Psalm. "The Lord is my shepherd," he says along with me, and then he just listens until the end. "And I shall dwell in the house of the Lord forever."

It is not long afterward that a priest from the church in Brooklyn calls to let me know that Ted has died. Very peacefully, at home. I tell her what a fine job I think her church did with Ted. She says they all loved him. I call the telephone company. There's no need to bother about the bill now, they say. We just cut off service when someone dies.

♦

LIES IN THE CITY

♦

"THERE'S A YOUNG MAN over here who's just lost his father. He's pretty upset, and I think he's on the level." It's David, my colleague, calling me in my office across the street from the church. I go over. And I think the guy's on the level, too. His father, who lived by himself in northern New Jersey, has just died of a heart attack. The son has been on a Greyhound bus all night to get here from North Carolina. He is exhausted and teary. He hasn't had much contact with his dad over the years, and is distraught at his sudden loss of ever having the opportunity to change that. He needs bus fare to Passaic. I can do that. We shake hands, and I tell him I'm sorry about his dad. He straightens up, thanks me, and heads uptown to the Port Authority to catch a bus.

"I'm getting my check from the V.A. on Thursday. They owe me from the beginning of the year, so it should be a big one. So I'll come in on Friday and pay you what I owe you. Without fail."

I look at the man sitting in the chair across my desk and I realize that I don't know whether he is Mr. McDougall or Mr. Gorman or Mr. Linz. I can never keep them straight. They're all about the same age. They even look sort of alike to me, or maybe I just think that because they all have the same story—a large check whose arrival is imminent. The other thing that they all have in common is that none of them has ever come in on Friday to pay me what he owes me. What has happened, I surmise, is that a pension or disability check has run out too soon. For some reason, they are ashamed to tell me that. Maybe they're afraid I will think they don't plan well. Or that they drank it away. Maybe they *did* drink it away. Maybe only one or two of them did. Or maybe it is just too hard to face the fact that their incomes are not large enough to stretch the whole month. And that they never will be. And that there's no way these guys are going to make it except by asking for help. And that this is not going to change. Maybe that's too much to face. So there's always a big check coming on Thursday. For whatever reason, they have concluded that the truth will not suffice. So they all tell the same lie.

"The people I'm working for on Long Island are going to let me stay in their house while they're away. But they're not gone yet. I don't know exactly *when* they're going to go, and in the meantime I need funds for carfare to get to work." Janet never uses the word "money." It's always "funds." I look at her. Her legs are thickly bandaged. She suffers from cellulitis, an inflammation of the lower extremities caused by poor circulation. It's common among homeless people because they often sleep sitting up. I once had her hospitalized for it against her will because her legs had become gangrenous. The smell of her decaying flesh that day was so strong that it lingered in my office for hours after she was gone. She recovered, and she kept her legs, but she walks with difficulty. She was very angry at me about this incident, and yet she welcomed my visits to the hospital. I still don't understand that. She will admit to no pain in her legs, though they are usually swollen and sometimes covered with weeping sores. She wears large sunglasses at all times, although an ophthalmologist in the hospital found nothing wrong with her eyes. I've never seen her drunk, but sometimes I can smell alcohol on her breath. Her story is never the same twice, but it always involves money—I mean *funds*—for getting to an unspecified job, and unnamed "people" who extend free housing to her. There is no way anybody would give Janet a job. There is no job she could do. Sometimes she can barely walk. As always, I refer her to John Heuss House drop-in center. As always, she refuses to go. She says she is not homeless and she is not mentally ill. Although she is both, I don't argue with her. I try another tack.

"You know, Janet, the people at John Heuss can help

you with your entitlements. I think you should consider public assistance. You shouldn't be trying to work with those legs in the shape they're in. You would get a check every month, something you could really depend on, and we could work on getting you an apartment. You could see a doctor. Joan over there is very knowledgeable about the welfare system, and I know she'd be glad to help. Why don't we call her?" I think this is an excellent speech. It has words like "check" and "apartment" in it as bait. It is also the gospel truth. But Janet doesn't bite.

"No, I don't think so. You have to wait in line so long."

"Well, only at first. Then they can deposit your check directly into the bank. It would be very convenient for you. You'd need some I.D. to get started, and Joan could help you."

When I mention I.D., Janet shakes her head. Then I remember that she often uses other names—she's been Sarah Barrett and Jane Goodman. Janet Wayne—the name I know—is probably not her real name, either. That's why she can't produce identification. She's not unique in this. Some of the mentally ill homeless are really someone else. Why? Some of them are schizophrenic, like Janet, and have lost track of who they once were. Some have had trouble with the law. And some are just ashamed of being homeless. And will go without money and medical help they desperately need in order not to have to document who they are.

And some are just con artists. How long will T.C. go on like this, I wonder as he sits down in the chair across from my desk. I know his real name because I've talked to his mother on the phone and I've seen his birth certificate. But he has presented himself to my colleagues as Al Smith, Mike Joseph, Mike Banks, and a couple of others. He tells elaborate stories of losing money or being robbed, of people being after him for money he owes. His life is lived enough on the wild side that any one of them could be true. But not all of them. Not all in the same week. I think of the boy who cried wolf, and hope this kid never really needs anything. He wants to go to California. A friend out there says he can stay with him. I call his mother, who has been taken in by her son so many times that she will only communicate with him through me. She's afraid to give him her telephone number. I tell her about California. She sighs. It's no solution, we agree, but maybe it's better than New York. Nothing else we've tried has worked, and he's going nowhere fast here. She sends a money order for the bus fare. I go to the bus station and buy a nonrefundable ticket. I tell T.C. that I want him to send me a card from Monterey so I know he got there okay and can tell his mom. I also tell him that I'm going to cut him up in tiny little pieces if he doesn't go. No card arrives. One of his friends tells me he's seen him uptown. You can sell those nonrefundable tickets, he says. But this friend also sometimes tells me things that aren't true. Especially about T.C. He likes to get T.C. into trouble. T.C. makes up lies about him, too, so they're more or less even. So I'm hoping that T.C. is in Monterey now and has just lost my address.

"You know, half of these people are liars," someone says to me. "Why do you let them lie to you?" Well, to begin with, I don't "let" them lie. They do it themselves. Besides, if there's one thing I've learned in this line of work it's that the truth doesn't always come out of people's mouths but it always comes out. Someone may lie to me about the nature of a need—to conceal an addiction, for instance, or to conceal an emotional illness—but he cannot lie about the fact that he *is* in need. Maybe not of what he's asking for, but he's in need of something. Any fool could see that. People whose lives are working out okay don't come to churches for money. Only people in need do that. So why should I back off when people lie to me about what they need? It may be that an opportunity will present itself to do something that will really be of help. Much of the time, that something won't be what the person asked for. Janet didn't want to go to the hospital. She wanted money. But she needed to go. She would have died if she hadn't gone. So I did something she didn't want me to do. And I'd do it again. And she knows it. Which is probably why she doesn't tell me when her legs hurt. She doesn't want to go to the drop-in center, either; she wants some money. But she *needs* to go. And maybe someday she will. In the meantime, she stops by every once in a while and tells me lies. I don't want to become so well-defended against lies that I am unable to respond to unexpected truth. I want to be free to see it if it's there. The price for that freedom is that sometimes you get burned.

Another call from David. Can you come over to the church? There's a young man here who has lost his father. I go across the street. The man's father lived by himself in northern New Jersey. He died suddenly of a heart attack. The son is exhausted from a night on a Greyhound bus from North Carolina. He hasn't seen much of his dad since he was little. He cries a bit as he talks about not ever having the chance to mend fences with his dad. He needs bus fare to Passaic.

At first, neither of us recognizes the other. I see a lot of people, and I guess he does, too. We both begin to realize that we have been here before at about the same time—somewhere around Passaic. His story trails off. "I'm sorry to hear this," I say. "I just needed to tell somebody," he says. He straightens up and we shake hands. And I am really sorry about his dad. And about everything.

♦

YOU LOOK TERRIFIC

♦

"SHE LOOKS SO PRETTY," my daughter says, as we watch a friend walk across the room at a party. Our friend has just broken off a long relationship with a man, and has changed her hairstyle. Her lipstick color, too, I think. "I do that," says my daughter. "I do something different to my appearance when I feel sad. Or I buy something new to wear. It makes me feel better."

I knew a young woman who dyed her hair jet black during a period in her life when she was unhappy and unsure of herself. And a man whose wife had died who appeared, suddenly, in a very obvious toupee. And hosts of seafarers when I worked on the waterfront, guys who grew beards and mustaches and sideburns while they were at sea, away from their families. Sometimes they were unfaithful to their wives, distracting themselves from their loneliness with women they met in port. I would never behave that way at home, they would say. I'm a different person at sea. I'm not really myself. When their contracts were fulfilled, they would shave off their beards or mustaches and go home.

Maybe you can become someone else by looking different. Maybe you don't have to be a widower who has lost his partner of forty years; maybe you can be a middle-aged guy with hair, someone to whom that didn't happen. Maybe you don't have to be a high school senior who is afraid she won't make it in college; maybe you can be an exotic Latin beauty with no visible means of support. I am a devoted husband and father with short hair; I don't know *who* this bearded Lothario is. I can't endure what is going on. There is no way out. But perhaps I can disappear, change the face I present to the world so much that the inside changes with it. Maybe I can look like what I wish I were.

Maybe you don't have to get old. You can go to a doctor who will pull your cheeks back around behind your ears and sew them in place. You'll look sort of like a puppet for a while, but you won't have any wrinkles, and in the right kind of soft light you'll look pretty darned young. You don't have to be flat-chested or thin-lipped or double-chinned, either. You can have all these things fixed, and you can be what you wish you were. What you used to be.

People used to wear black for a full year when somebody in their family had died. Everyone could tell at a glance that they were bereaved, and could make allowances for them. We don't do that today. We say it's because such things are morbid, but it's really because we find it difficult to admit that there are still things that can't be fixed in a few days. We don't want a uniform for our grief. That would be acknowledging its permanence. We want to get out of it as soon as we can. So we paper over our heartaches after a week or two, and everyone around us soon forgets we had them. "You look terrific," they say. And we can only answer, "Oh, I feel fine." Even if we feel like dying.

I think of the homeless women I know. Most of those who have children became homeless because of economic circumstances beyond their control. The majority of those who are single and childless, though, are also mentally ill. I am often struck by the importance of clothing and accessories in some of those women's lives: intricate arrangements of jewelry they have fashioned from string and soda-can tabs, carefully arranged layers of clothing they have found in the trash, chosen with attention to color. I remember giving a woman a tiny amount of money for food. When I saw her the next week she showed me a fake-pearl bracelet she had bought with some of the money. She had no home. She had no money. She was out of food again. But she had spent almost a dollar for the bracelet. I remember another who asked for a lipstick when I inquired what she needed during a hospital stay. A lipstick and some underwear that was new and pretty. I look terrible, she said.

I want to cry about this. I know what it is to try and fix my broken self by fixing the way I look. I do it. My friend whose love affair has ended does it. The man whose wife has died does it. Most of us work our way back to ourselves, back to a place in which our lives are bearable again. We get better. We no longer try to dress ourselves up and out of our problems. But what about the woman who wanders the locked unit of Bellevue and needs a lipstick and some pretty underwear? And the lady in the pearl bracelet who has no food? To want to look nice in the face of such doom, such endless inner chaos, to want to look nice when one hears voices that aren't there—I am amazed by it. And appalled by it. I am torn between anger and admiration. You've got a lot more serious problems than looking terrible, I think. This is no time to be thinking about lipstick. You're not facing reality. If you're ever going to get better, you've got to start facing reality. You are ill. And yet you are so human. So like me. Trying so hard to look like what you wish you were. Trying to look like people look when they have bedrooms and health insurance and dry-cleaning tickets. Like sane people look.

Bob was a bond salesman on Wall Street. A few years ago he was making more money in a year than I'll ever see. A combination of manic-depressive illness and alcoholism robbed him of that life, and today he is a homeless man trying to survive the New York City streets. He sometimes gets jobs, but he cannot hold on to them. Once he even got a job back in the bond business, courtesy of a friend from the old days who compassionately but mistakenly thought a break was all Bob needed.

Bob's appearance mirrors the roller coaster of his illness. When he is in the grip of depression, he is dirty and his hair is unkempt. He wears overalls and a plaid shirt, the same clothes all the time. When he begins to soar into a manic state, a more energetic but equally dangerous one for him, he changes the way he looks. He finds a used suit. It fits. It's a Botany 500; Bob knows his brands. In the overkill that characterizes his illness, he finds three or four more, spending days roaming the city finding suits, finding shirts, finding ties. He even finds some yuppie suspenders with ducks on them. He finds a place to take a shower, finds leather shoes to replace the sneakers he's been wearing. He applies for jobs. He gets them; Bob is intelligent and well spoken. And a truly nice guy. Then he is frightened by this brush with the responsible world, afraid that he will not be able to maintain the tenuous balance between his highs and his lows, which the world of work will require of him. He becomes terribly anxious, begins to feel closed in, unable to remain in the same room for very long. He self-medicates with alcohol. And soon things fall apart. It has happened before.

"You look terrific," people have been telling me lately. I am changing jobs, going from one that was full of frustration to one that I know will not be. I have started wearing makeup again, and stopped wearing the same three outfits all the time. I wear earrings again. I look at a picture of myself that was taken shortly before I made this employment decision, a time when people were saying to me, "You look tired." They were too kind to say I looked like hell, but I had mirrors at home. Dark circles under my eyes that I didn't bother to conceal. No lips. No eyelashes. Gray skin. Hair with no shape. I'm fine, I would answer, I'm just a little tired. But I looked like I was dying. Maybe I was. I scared people, looking like that.

Bob is back, in dirty hair and sneakers and the same old overalls, smelling of old sweat and fresh despair. "You look terrific," he says. Thanks, I say, I'm feeling a lot better. You look tired, Bob, I tell him. He knows he looks like hell. I give him a cup of coffee and ask him how he is. His eyes rarely meet mine as he tonelessly recites the history of his latest unraveling. When they do, they are black pools of pain. Neither of us mentions the new clothes. Some of them still hang in my office for safekeeping. He worked so hard putting them together. He wanted so much to look like the person he used to be. I remember him coming in with the suits on a hanger. Could he keep these here for a while? He had put on a jacket to show me the fit. "Bill Blass," he had said, showing me the label. "How do I look?"

"You look terrific," I had said.

BEFORE THE LAST WAR

IT IS JANUARY 14, 1991, the day before the deadline set by the United Nations for a withdrawal of Iraqi troops from Kuwait. Everyone is hoping that something will happen to stop us from attacking Iraq. Surely the professionals on both sides have this one in hand, and what we are seeing is just saber rattling, which neither party really means. Probably they're about to settle, and we just can't be told anything until it's over. An expensive gesture on our part, of course, but one supposes that this buildup of hardware and personnel on the border between Iraq and Saudi Arabia serves to demonstrate our seriousness. Surely it is not for actual *use*.

Trinity Church is having a vigil for peace. Musicians and speakers, all day. People from the mayor's office and the stock exchange. Some famous musicians—Ruth Laredo is playing, and Anthony Newman. An imam is coming from an uptown mosque, to pray to Allah in Arabic that there not be a war. A rabbi is there, and a monsignor. Some Quaker teenagers who have a jazz band are playing. Between numbers, one of them speaks soberly about kids a year older than himself being over there. A jazz pianist plays and sings something sad and beautiful about the beauty of the earth. A string ensemble plays Samuel Barber's "Adagio for Strings." Surely that is the saddest piece of music ever composed, I think as I walk down the side aisle. The church is full of people; they are all very quiet, just listening. Some of them pray. Some light candles. One woman, who wears a corsage made of an American flag and a bunch of yellow ribbons, cries in her pew. I stop to talk to her. She tells me her son is over there and she is so afraid.

I stand in the aisle and talk in a whisper with her for a few minutes. Then I go back outside. I've been out in front of the church all morning, and just came in for a little while to get warm. Jack and Sara have been out there all day, too. They are both painters. Jack is also a priest. We've been inviting passersby to stop and paint their prayers for peace on canvas screens in front of the church.

It was rough getting started on this paint-your-own-prayers thing at seven-thirty this morning. Wall Street was busy even at that hour, people on their way to the exchanges to see if they'd made money while they slept, people working the crowd already with handbills about foot doctors and topless bars, homeless people shuffling along the sidewalk toward the church and a seat inside, out of the cold. But most stockbrokers had more urgent things on their minds than painting graffiti on a church, and the homeless had had a long night. Painting prayers for peace was not selling very well. Fine. I would just start by myself, and hope a Tom Sawyer effect would kick in.

"GRANT US YOUR PEACE," I painted in blue in the middle of the canvas. I retraced the letters in red, hoping it would look like each letter had a red shadow. It didn't, but at least I had begun. And, turning around, I saw my first customer, a Puerto Rican transvestite from the neighborhood. Paint a prayer for peace *en español*, I said. She smiled and took the brush I held out to her. With a few expert strokes she made a beautiful blue dove bearing a yellow banner in her beak reading "POR LA PAZ." I was amazed at her talent, and told her so. She waved her thanks and went inside. Fifteen minutes later he came back out, dressed like a man, and walked off down the street.

Then a homeless man came up and asked what I was doing to the church. I told him about the prayers for peace, and he started in on a big yellow sun, with "GOD BE WITH US ALL" underneath it in green. Sara arrived, surveyed the canvas and filled in the area between my clumsy letters and the dove with some fat horizontal strokes of blue. She is an abstract expressionist. I engaged a Dutch couple in a conversation about the war. They wrote a line from a Dutch hymn next to the homeless man's sun, telling me that it was about all of us being children of God. Then a Chinese man stopped to ask Jack for directions, and agreed to paint the character for "peace."

All in all, the morning has gone well. By now, most of the canvas panels are full. There are prayers for peace in Italian, in Greek, in Japanese, in Urdu, in Arabic. There is a brown gingerbread boy with "LET THE CHILDREN LIVE" on his stomach in yellow. Sara jumps in now and then with her horizontal lines, and the whole thing seems to hang together pretty well. Incredibly—this is New York City, after all—none of the messages are aggressive or obscene. They are quiet and prayerful, full of hope. People of all ages and persuasions paint on the canvas as if it were important that they do so, as if the pictures and words could make peace happen. The afternoon continues cold. Our feet and hands are like blocks of ice, and we take turns ducking inside now and then to listen to the music and get warm. Always at the back of our minds is the deadline. Tomorrow night we may be at war, says Jack. Nah, we all think. It's not really going to happen.

And it doesn't. Not that night. We close the doors to the church at six o'clock. The prayers for peace look festive on the canvas screens behind the big iron gate, as if there isn't too much to worry about, as if they had already worked. We go home and listen to the news. Mostly it's television anchorpeople telling each other they don't know much.

Two days later we're in church again. The Task Force Against Racism is putting together announcements of a conference we're planning. We are eating pizza and stuffing envelopes when Father Sabune appears at the door. Don't just stand there, we say, come on in and make yourself useful. But he doesn't come in, and he doesn't smile. He stays in the doorway. And he says the war has started. We're bombing Baghdad right now. My God, somebody says, and then nobody speaks for a few moments. We stand up and hold hands in a circle. Somebody starts the Lord's Prayer. When it is finished, most of us are in tears. Somebody brings in a radio, and we listen to the news. It's still mostly broadcasters telling each other they don't know much. But we are at war now. We put on our coats and start for home.

Outside in the dark, the prayers for peace are still brave on the canvas panels in front of the church. The dove with her banner. The homeless man's big yellow sun. The gingerbread boy with the sign on his stomach. "LET THE CHILDREN LIVE." The sky over Manhattan is dark and silent. Half the population of Baghdad is under seventeen.

♦

LOVE ME TENDER, AURA LEE

♦

SOMETHING IS WRONG with my husband. I can tell because he is dashing from the kitchen to the dining room and back with a mighty scowl on his face. I slink into the kitchen to catch him on a return dash and see if I can find out what it is. He reenters. Without meeting my gaze he approaches the sink. "I don't know why people have to leave half a bowl of Cheerios in the sink," he says grimly. I can narrow down the "people" to whom he refers: they can only be my daughter and me. We're the only other people who live here, and somehow I don't get the sense that he is referring to himself just now. I don't eat Cheerios. So it must be Anna. Anna must be the people we're talking about. I look into the sink. There are about thirty-five hapless Cheerios in the sink strainer. Amazing how they hold their shape, I think to myself. "Half a very *small* bowl," I say to my husband. He doesn't think that's very funny. He is appalled at the way we waste food. I am appalled that he even notices. Don't you have anything better to do than count Cheerios, I say silently. I feel better when I say things like that to myself. He makes me feel guilty with his Cheerio counts. He also counts grains of rice. "You're throwing away enough to feed an army," he says. The army of Lilliput, I think. And I feel better again.

I wish I had been brought up in the Depression like he was. Then I would save things, too, instead of throwing them out the way I do. But I wasn't. I was a child of the fifties. We just didn't have a head of steam about leftover food. My mother *did* talk about starving children in other lands to make me eat. But they didn't seem very real. I rarely had the experience of wanting something and not having it. Our life-style was not extravagant: we didn't have two cars or take fancy vacations. But it was comfortable. We never went without anything we needed.

But wait a minute. Neither did he. He had a much more privileged childhood than I did, in fact. But need was in the air when he was little. And plenty was in the air when I was. Kids in the thirties just knew that times were hard. And we just knew that there was more than enough to go around. And it has made us profoundly different from each other. He counts Cheerios and I don't. I have been known to throw away pennies when cleaning out a drawer. He is really sorry I ever told him that. He feels terrible when the milk sours and I pour it down the sink. When I first met him, I looked in his refrigerator one day and found six or seven partial quarts of soured milk. He was holding on to it, he explained, because you can use it to make waffles. You can also throw it out, I said. He looked pained. I always *make* sour milk when I need it, I said, by adding a teaspoon of vinegar to sweet milk. I never have to do that, he said. He made waffles with the sour milk. And sour-milk pancakes. Lots of them. I would make them again today, he says, if you'd just save the milk. But old habits die hard. Out it goes.

I remember a getting-to-know-you conversation early in our acquaintance. He said something about having served in Germany during the war. Which war, I wondered. Vietnam, I hoped. But it was Korea. Oh. I was *born* during the Korean War. I was beginning to understand that this man had suits older than I was. How can you be interested in someone who doesn't remember the Second World War, I have asked him a hundred times. I must seem very callow to you. No, he says. Why not, I ask. He says he doesn't know.

"I need to know about 'The Brady Bunch,' " he says one day. "My students are always talking about how their families are not like 'The Brady Bunch.' " I tell him what "The Brady Bunch" was. It was about a happy stepfamily in which the parents always knocked on their kids' bedroom doors and said "Can we come in?" Then they would come in and settle something really difficult in a heart-to-heart talk that lasted two minutes tops. While I'm at it I tell him about "Leave It to Beaver" and "Ozzie and Harriet." And "Mr. Ed." Who settled things in "Mr. Ed," he wants to know. The horse, usually, I say. I sing the theme song for him. I swear I'm not making any of this up, I say. I tell him I already know about Fibber McGee and Molly.

It is October 31, 1938. He is ten years old. His parents are out for the evening. Only he and the maid are home. She tells him to come into her room right now. They sit by the radio and listen to the announcer describe a spaceship that has landed near Princeton, New Jersey. A farmer describes the creatures that emerge from it. They listen in horror as a scientist describes the devastation in New York City. The invaders are making their way to Central Park. Many people have died.

Richard hears a buzzing noise outside in the sky. His heart pounds as he puts on his sweater and goes out in the yard. Looking up, he sees something moving across the black sky, something with blinking lights. He thinks that it may be a spaceship. He may be seeing the end of the world. He may never see his parents again.

It is October 1962. I am eleven years old. United States intelligence has detected Soviet missile bases in Cuba, weapons trained on our shores from a vantage point only ninety miles away. We have circled the island with a naval blockade, and President Kennedy has issued an ultimatum to Nikita Khrushchev: the missiles must leave Cuba or we will attack the Soviet Union with any means at our disposal, including nuclear weapons. Our teacher runs us through the air-raid drill: under the desk, knees under your chest, hands clasped behind your neck, head down, eyes closed. Do not open your eyes until I tell you, she says. If you hear an explosion, don't look at it. You will go blind if you look at it. Afterward, my best friend and I are waiting for her school bus home. We look at each other with tears in our eyes. "We may never see each other again," she whispers. I am too frightened to answer.

It is 1987. We are driving late at night. Elvis is singing "Love Me Tender" on the radio. I begin to sing along. Richard begins to sing along, too, but I notice he's singing different words, something about blackbirds in the spring. "What's that?" I ask. "Aura Lee," he answers, and goes into the refrain. Elvis and I harmonize with him at the end. "For my darling, I love you, and I always will." I didn't know there were other words to that song, I say. Neither did I, he says, and pats my hand.

FOR THE BEST IN PAPERBACKS, LOOK FOR THE 

In every corner of the world, on every subject under the sun, Penguin represents quality and variety—the very best in publishing today.

For complete information about books available from Penguin—including Pelicans, Puffins, Peregrines, and Penguin Classics—and how to order them, write to us at the appropriate address below. Please note that for copyright reasons the selection of books varies from country to country.

In the United Kingdom: For a complete list of books available from Penguin in the U.K., please write to *Dept E.P., Penguin Books Ltd, Harmondsworth, Middlesex, UB7 0DA.*

In the United States: For a complete list of books available from Penguin in the U.S., please write to *Consumer Sales, Penguin USA, P.O. Box 999—Dept. 17109, Bergenfield, New Jersey 07621-0120.* VISA and MasterCard holders call 1-800-253-6476 to order all Penguin titles.

In Canada: For a complete list of books available from Penguin in Canada, please write to *Penguin Books Canada Ltd, 10 Alcorn Avenue, Suite 300, Toronto, Ontario, Canada M4V 3B2.*

In Australia: For a complete list of books available from Penguin in Australia, please write to the *Marketing Department, Penguin Books Ltd, P.O. Box 257, Ringwood, Victoria 3134.*

In New Zealand: For a complete list of books available from Penguin in New Zealand, please write to the *Marketing Department, Penguin Books (NZ) Ltd, Private Bag, Takapuna, Auckland 9.*

In India: For a complete list of books available from Penguin, please write to *Penguin Overseas Ltd, 706 Eros Apartments, 56 Nehru Place, New Delhi, 110019.*

In Holland: For a complete list of books available from Penguin in Holland, please write to *Penguin Books Nederland B.V., Postbus 195, NL-1380AD Weesp, Netherlands.*

In Germany: For a complete list of books available from Penguin, please write to *Penguin Books Ltd, Friedrichstrasse 10-12, D-6000 Frankfurt Main 1, Federal Republic of Germany.*

In Spain: For a complete list of books available from Penguin in Spain, please write to *Longman, Penguin España, Calle San Nicolas 15, E-28013 Madrid, Spain.*

In Japan: For a complete list of books available from Penguin in Japan, please write to *Longman Penguin Japan Co Ltd, Yamaguchi Building, 2-12-9 Kanda Jimbocho, Chiyoda-Ku, Tokyo 101, Japan.*

814.54
Cra
2021

Crafton
Sewing room

CANA LIBRARY
Cana Lutheran Church
2119 Catalpa Drive
Berkley MI 48072-1899
(810) 543-0767

DEMCO